GRACE SUFFICIENT

© Copyright 2009 David J Randall

All rights reserved. No part of this publication may be reproduced, stored in a retrieval system, or transmitted in any form or by any means, electronic, mechanical, photocopying, recording or otherwise, without prior permission from the publishers.

Published by
Kachere Series
P.O. Box 1037, Zomba

ISBN 978-99908-87-59-4
Kachere Books no. 43

The Kachere Series is represented outside Africa by:
African Books Collective Oxford (orders@africanbookscollective.com)
Michigan State University Press East Lansing (msupress@msu.edu)

Layout and Cover design: Josephine Kawejere

Printed by Lightning Source

GRACE SUFFICIENT

DAVID J RANDALL

Kachere Books no. 43

Kachere Series
Zomba
2009

Kachere Series
P.O. Box 1037
Zomba
kachere@globemw.net
http/www.kachereseries.org/

This book is part of the Kachere Series, a range of books on religion, culture and society from Malawi. Other related Kachere books:

George Shepperson and Thomas Price, *Independent African, John Chilembwe and the Nyasaland Rising of 1915*, Kachere Monograph no. 13, 2000

Patrick Makondesa, *The Church History of Providence Industrial Mission 1900 – 1940*, Kachere Theses no. 5, 2006

Andrew C Ross, *Blantyre Mission and the Making of Modern Malawi*, Kachere Monograph no. 1, 1996

John McCracken, *Politics and Christianity in Malawi 1875-1940*, Kachere Monograph no. 8, 2000

Andrew C. Ross, *Colonialism to Cabinet Crisis: A Political History if Malawi*, Kachere Books no. 44, 2009

Rachel NyaGondwe Banda, *Women of the Bible and Culture: Baptist Convention Women in Southern Malawi*, Kachere Theses no. 3, 2005

Helen E P van Koevering, *Dancing their Dreams: The Lakeshore Nyanja Women of the Anglican Diocese of Niassa*, Kachere Theses no. 9, 2005.

Klaus Fiedler, *The Gospel Takes Roots on Kilimanjaro: A History of the Evangelical Lutheran Church of Old Moshi-Mbokomu 1885 – 1940*, Kachere Monograph no. 23, 2006

Desmond Dudwa Phiri, *Let us Fight for Africa, A Play on the Chilembwe Rising*, Kachere book no. 31, 2007

Series Editors: R. Likupe, J.C. Chakanza, F.L. Chingota, Klaus Fiedler, P.A. Kalilombe, Chimwemwe Katumbi, S. Mohammad, François Nsengiyumva, M. Ott

Contents

Foreword: by the Reverend Professor Ken Ross, General Secretary
            of the World Mission Council of the Church of Scotland   v

Chapter 1 – The Person   1

Chapter 2 – The Child   7

Chapter 3 – The Missionary   16

Chapter 4 – The Daughter   23

Chapter 5 – The Nurse   26

Chapter 6 – The Tutor   35

Chapter 7 – The Correspondent   48

Chapter 8 – The Diarist   54

Chapter 9 – The Hostess   61

Chapter 10 – The Patient   73

Foreword

Elizabeth Mantell would have been amazed, and probably appalled, to find that her biography had been written. A woman of profound humility, she would instinctively shun the limelight. This is one good reason why her story has to be told. Self-effacing as she was, she made a deep impression on many people. There was an integrity of character and authenticity of faith that made even the most mundane encounter with Elizabeth an uplifting experience. On one occasion we were travelling in the north of Malawi, a family group of six. We paid a visit to Ekwendeni and then proceeded northwards. After about an hour we experienced a problem with our vehicle and ended up limping back into Ekwendeni as dusk was falling. We met Liz on her way home from the hospital where she worked. Was there any possibility that she could put us up for the night? "Grace" is just the right word to describe her response. Many others would have similar stories to tell.

It is a well known fact of history that there has been a particularly strong relationship between Scotland and Malawi. Government, church and civil society remain active today in building on the links and associations which began with David Livingstone's celebrated travels in the mid-nineteenth century. There are many strands to the remarkable relationship between the two nations but it is the people involved who have made it what it is. The personal relationships formed between individuals and families are the sinews which keep the relationship functioning. It would be hard to find a better illustration of this point than the life of Elizabeth Mantell. The pages of this book are alive with the love which Elizabeth had for Malawian friends and colleagues and the love which they had for her.

The book helps to fill a major gap in the literature on church and mission in Malawi. Women missionaries have been numerous and influential. Yet, on the whole, they have done their work without seeking or receiving much in the way of public recognition. Leadership positions, and the consequent biographies, have been largely monopolised by men. It is high time for the contribution of women missionaries to the growth of Christianity in Malawi to be more extensively considered and celebrated. One way to do this is to focus on the life of a particular individual. This biography of Elizabeth will shed light on an area that is ripe for research and reflection.

It will hold particular interest because of the period which it covers. Much has been written about the pioneering days of missionary work in Malawi, the 1875-1914 period. Very little has been written about missionaries of recent times. With the advent of post-colonialism, missionaries went out of fashion. National pride might celebrate a David Livingstone or a Mary Slessor but there is little expectation that the missionary vocation will find expression in contemporary times. Elizabeth's service was offered in the last third of the 20th century. To have the opportunity to get inside her thinking and motivation is the prospect offered by this enticing biography.

The book also makes an original contribution to the story of one of the famous centres of mission work in Malawi. Ekwendeni was among the first mission stations to be established and has continued to be prominent in the work of Livingstonia Synod right up to the present day. It has had a particular orientation to medical mission, the sphere in which Elizabeth found her forte. The vision for mission work to include the healing dimension of the ministry of Christ is one which has inspired many over the years. A close study of how one woman worked out this particular vocation is a welcome addition to the literature.

Above all, however, it is the devotional aspect of the missionary calling which is described and celebrated in this book. This is something often overlooked, yet it is the true spring of missionary life and service. It is not easy to discern and discuss the spirituality which is the deep, driving force of a missionary's life. This is what David Randall has attempted in this book and he writes with both insight and sensitivity. A pastor's eye allows him to see the inner life of prayer which others might easily fail to observe. He gently lifts the lid both on the growth of Elizabeth's own faith and the missionary motivation which moved her, retiring as she was, to share her faith with others wherever she went. The book serves as a continuation of this humble yet resolute witness. It may be that even Elizabeth herself would countenance its publication if she knew that it would prove to be a testimony to the sufficiency of the grace of God.

Kenneth R. Ross
General Secretary of the
World Mission Council of Church of Scotland
Edinburgh, October 2007

Chapter 1
The Person

The daylight was fading but Elizabeth suggested that we take a walk before dinner. It was a late afternoon in August 1996 when we walked out from her house in Ekwendeni. Although her terminal illness must have been working in her by that time, she strode out, leading us past the rough field which serves as a football pitch. We came eventually to a settlement of a few simple houses, one of which Elizabeth planned to visit.

A Malawian lady came to the door and, after a brief exchange, my wife and I were informed that we too might enter. The interior of the house was dark and bare; there were few home comforts. On a mattress on the floor lay an elderly woman who was clearly very ill.

My wife and I were introduced to the mother and daughter and then sat in silence while Elizabeth spoke with them in Tumbuka. After a while she reached into her bag and brought out her Tumbuka Bible. In the dim light she read a passage and then prayed with the dying lady, before again reaching into her bag, this time to produce a bag of sugar which she gave to the woman and her daughter.

Soon we were on our way again, resuming our late-afternoon stroll, before heading back to Elizabeth's house for dinner.

This scene remains vivid in the memory. We had witnessed what generations of missionaries had been doing in Malawi over the years. The house showed little evidence that it existed at the end of the twentieth century; we could have been accompanying Robert Laws, David Livingstone or any of the other luminaries who served the people of Nyasaland/Malawi over the century and a half since missionaries had first set foot in this part of what was then known as the Dark Continent.

Elizabeth would have been surprised, even horrified, to hear her name bracketed with those of such celebrities. As will be emphasised in this account of her life, one of her characteristics was an endearing lack of any apparent realisation of just how special a person she was. When people suggested to her, as we frequently did, that she should have written a book about her experiences, her response was: "And what would I write? '...Got up in the morning...worked all day at the hospital...went home...'?" What she would not do herself, this book will attempt: to tell something of the story of an unassuming Scottish missionary who was respected and loved by a remarkably large circle of friends and admirers, both in Scotland and in Malawi.

The bag from which Elizabeth drew out her Bible and the sugar reminded us of the twin commands of the Lord whom she sought to serve: to minister to both the souls and the bodies of other people. She was not one to emphasise either to the exclusion of the other; she would not have given her dying friend the Bible verses and prayer without the sugar; nor would she have given the sugar alone. Her concern was with the spiritual and the physical; this was, of course, the story of her life as a medical missionary. She was not only a nursing sister and tutor, nor merely an evangelist, but both together. Billy Graham has said that we are to go to needy people with the gospel in one hand and a cup of cold water in the other; Elizabeth's bag of sugar was better than a cup of cold water, but the principle was the same. She instinctively practised holistic care, before it had become popular to use that term.

Elizabeth's concern always was to merge physical and spiritual care, and this was the true not only when she was in Malawi. As her pastor, I remember visiting her a year after her final return to Scotland when she was terminally ill in Aberdeen Royal Infirmary. She was in one of those four-bedded rooms, which actually give less privacy than the old-fashioned Florence Nightingale-style, long ward. Feeling that she couldn't say very much without being overheard, she slipped me a note which she had scribbled on an old envelope. I still have it. It said:

> "The lady next to me was asking about 'faith' today. She feels there is no hope and I was sharing with her. I would like to give her a book that she might find helpful – light and not too daunting. Could you find something for me. Thanks. Eliz."

As we talked on, without referring openly to her request, I felt as if I were involved in some clandestine operation. In due course I provided something suitable, and I have no knowledge of what happened thereafter. The incident reveals the fact that Elizabeth was not a missionary only when she stepped off the plane at Lilongwe. Her desire was to care for people wherever she found them. Whether it was during their dying days in a little hut in Ekwendeni or during her own illness in a highly-equipped hospital in

Aberdeen, she would seek to follow the way of the Master who had called her and whom she loved to serve.

Who then was this unassuming and highly respected nurse? What brought her to Malawi? It is the purpose of these pages to tell something of that story, the story she did not want to tell herself, a story which she would have wished dedicated - like the stained glass window in her home church in Macduff - to the glory of God. This window was dedicated on 22nd April 1998 at a special service attended by family and friends. It bears the inscription:

> "To the glory of God and in memory of Elizabeth Mantell, medical missionary in Malawi from 1966 – 1972 and 1982 – 1996".

The window, depicting Elizabeth in nursing uniform, holding a Malawian baby, was designed and made by Jennifer-Jane Bayliss of Abbey Studio, Fintray, near Aberdeen. In style it combines the traditional with the contemporary. It links the church in Ekwendeni and the church in Macduff, by combining the Celtic style of the inter-linked border, suggesting the eternal being of God, with the colorful African style of the central design. Through the design runs the text which meant so much to Elizabeth and which was given her at her valedictory service before her return to Malawi in 1982: "My grace is sufficient for you". That grace was Elizabeth's strength.

Donations towards the cost of the window had come from near and far. Nearly 70 individuals or groups contributed to its installation. Among the donors' comments were the following:

- From Jean in Glasgow: "I worked with Liz at Mulanje Hospital in 1967/68 and this was the beginning of a friendship covering the next thirty years. I have many happy memories of a lovely person".

- From Mary, in Edinburgh: "Elizabeth and my husband shared a General Assembly breakfast platform/table when we were both home from Malawi and Lausanne between 1989 – 93, and, following Elizabeth's appeal for vests for her premature babies, my Guild ladies knitted enthusiastically and the two boxes of vests went to Malawi, via Scotland and Stagecoach".

- From Joan in Hampshire: "Elizabeth and I started our nursing careers together in August 1960. She was a wonderful nurse – thorough and gentle in everything she did. We were very close friends and she has been an inspiration to us too in our Christian faith".

- From Alex in Forres: "I was born in Bandawe, Malawi in 1907, where my parents had been among the earliest missionaries. It is good to keep names such as Miss Mantell's before our churches in all the changes of our age".

- From Isobel and Gordon in Tarves: "My wife and I got to know and respect Liz when I did a six-month locumship in Ekwendeni. She was an inspiration to all who came in contact with her".

- From Shena in Glasgow: "Memories of Elizabeth will live on in our hearts, but the window will be a lasting tribute to someone who gave her whole life to caring for others".

Elizabeth occupied a special place in the long story of the link between Scotland and Malawi and her name will surely be remembered with affection and thanksgiving to her Lord and ours in both countries. Interestingly, that long association has been boosted by the recent inauguration of the Scotland-Malawi Partnership under the auspices of the Scottish Government. At such a time, it is good to remember that such partnership follows on many years of connection between Malawi and Scotland. Elizabeth Mantell was part of that story.

As mentioned already, a New Testament text is woven diagonally through the whole design of the window. That text is 2 Corinthians 12:9: "My grace is sufficient for you". The apostle Paul had been praying that God would remove his "thorn in the flesh" (whatever it was). God's answer was that he would not remove it but would give Paul special grace to cope with it.

Elizabeth had adopted these words as her life-text; she would frequently refer to them and to the strength which she derived from keeping them in her heart and soul. This explains the choice of *Grace Sufficient* as the title of this account of her life. Just as the words of the text dominate the design of the memorial window, so Elizabeth's life was shot through with the theme, that of 'grace sufficient'.

The words feature in one of the hymns of Keith Getty and Stuart Townend. That hymn was published in 2005 and so was never known by Elizabeth, but the theme celebrated in the hymn was very much part of her life:

> Hope that lifts me from despair;
> Love that casts out every fear
> As I stand on every promise of Your word.

> Not forsaken, not alone,
> For the Comforter has come
> And I stand on every promise of Your word.
>
> Grace sufficient, grace for me;
> Grace for all who will believe.
> We will stand on every promise of Your word.

Elizabeth took her stand on God's promises and especially on this Word about His all-sufficient grace.

Reference will be made several times to Dr Robert Laws and his pioneering work in Malawi, then Nyasaland, as chronicled by my own late minister, Rev. Hamish McIntosh in his book, *Robert Laws: Servant of Africa* (published by Handsel Press & Central Africana in 1993). When Dr Laws died, a columnist in the Glasgow Evening Citizen, writing under the pen-name of "Churchman", said of him,

> "Nothing impressed me more about Dr Laws than his humility. He was a great man who was unconscious of his greatness"

These words might also be said of Elizabeth, who had absolutely no notion of how special a person she was, or of the immensely high regard in which many people held her. Iain Craighead, a General Practitioner who fulfilled his elective study at Ekwendeni in 1992, speaks for many in writing:

> "I only knew Elizabeth for a comparatively short time but she certainly made a deep impression on me."

This doctor referred to Elizabeth's cook, Henderson, as being

> "Unhappy about cooking porridge in the morning because he felt it was a food unsuitable for someone of Elizabeth's high social standing."

Those who knew her can probably imagine what Elizabeth's response to such an assessment would have been!

But, whatever might be said about her social standing, a subject in which she would have had no interest, it was the quality of her personal, professional and spiritual life that left its mark. I have had it in mind for a long time to write her story; at times I have wondered whether I had left it too late, but the thought has refused to go away. In the course of gathering information from friends and colleagues of Elizabeth, I have uncovered more about the very high regard in which she was held. I am most grateful to all who have contributed their reminiscences and recollections and have included excerpts from most.

Typical of the many letters received was one from George Martin, who taught at Kamuzu Academy from 1987 to 1992: "Thanks for asking - I have really enjoyed pausing to think about her again". Similarly, Lindsey Malcolm, who taught in Ekwendeni Girls' High School in 1987/8 and lived "on the other side of Liz's house, through the adjoining door", thanked me "for allowing me to evoke some memories of such a friend". Many people have said similar things, and it is hoped that this account of her life will be a blessing to all who read it.

She herself, as many have recognised and as Kenneth Ross has pointed out in his Foreword, would have been horrified at the thought of a book being written about her. Even should she have become reconciled to the idea, she would not have wanted any such biography to 'praise her to the skies'. She would have agreed with the following words by a missionary in Thailand, quoted by Nancy Dimmock in *Women in Mission*:

> "The idea that missionaries are haloed saints, mature and perfected, above the sins of most mortals and so not needing much prayer, has done great disservice to the missionary cause. If you ever lived with missionaries, you would know that their haloes are askew. If I were to say that a missionary preaches the Gospel, may (if female) put curlers in her hair, likes ice-cream, travels a lot, longs for letters from home, can be thoughtless or domineering or depressed, perspires, has cakes that don't always rise, never gets beyond the need of the Lord's teaching ... and feels irritable in the heat, your first thought would be, 'Sounds like a description of me'. Exactly. Yet our glamourisation of missionaries blinds us to their need of down-to-earth prayer for down-to-earth details"

I remember conducting a missionary retreat, which Elizabeth arranged at a place called Chikangawa. One of the themes expressed was a desire that the public would treat missionaries as ordinary people, not spiritual superheroes who occupy a higher plane. One spoke of the embarrassment of receiving the kind of letters from home that include sentiments on the lines of: "You're so wonderful…"

Elizabeth would agree with all of that – and yet she *was* a special person! Part of that specialness was her complete lack of any awareness of it.

Chapter 2
The Child

Elizabeth was born on 24th June 1941 at Kasama in Northern Rhodesia, now Zambia.

Her father, Henry Percy Mantell, commonly known as Percy, was born in England of an English father and a Welsh mother. As a young man he went to Central Africa to work for the African Lakes Corporation. This was a well-established trading company, originally incorporated in June 1878 as the Livingstonia Central Africa Company. According to a cutting in the possession of Percy's son, Harry (there is no record of the date or source of the cutting), the company was formed by:

> "A number of philanthropic gentlemen who had been impressed by David Livingstone's plea for the establishment of regular trade routes and the introduction of lawful commerce whereby the slave trade – that curse of Central Africa – might be exterminated and security obtained for the life and property of the native inhabitants"

Two Scottish brothers, John and Fred Moir, who had contemplated beginning a similar venture, were appointed joint managers; they set out in 1878 to develop the work. There was much opposition from slave-traders, in the course of which both John and Fred were wounded. Fred was shot through the right arm; the bone was shattered and, on his return home, it was found necessary to remove the elbow joint. The operation was so successful that, in later years, Fred was reportedly able to play excellent games of golf and billiards. It is also reported that Fred had a working knowledge of three continental and three African languages. Unfortunately the article I saw about John Moir was written in one of these languages, with no translation!

Ultimately the slave trade was suppressed; the same newspaper cutting makes the comment that, although the company did, in fact, make profits and earn dividends for its shareholders,

> "A notable feature of the company is that it is probably the only trading or transport business ever formed not for the express purpose of making money but rather to fulfil the humanitarian objectives of its

initiators – namely, the abolition of the slave trade and bestowal of freedom and safety of the natives"

The company was for a time known as Mandala which, in the local language, means "shine". This was apparently because of the reflection of the sunlight off John's spectacles. The name Mandala came to be used to designate any trading station and is still seen in Malawi on garages and vans. Many years later, when Elizabeth's half-sister Ruth was attending a meeting in Dundee in connection with the Tell Scotland movement, she found herself in conversation with a lady. The talk turned to Africa and Ruth mentioned that her father had worked for the African Lakes Corporation, whereupon the lady (the daughter of one of the Moir brothers) remarked: "My father *was* the African Lakes Corporation"!

The company developed and eventually had 12 trading stations and a staff of about 100 Europeans. One of them was Percy Mantell, who worked for about a year with African Lakes before deciding to move to the United States. Three months of American life was enough for him, however, and he moved back to the African Lakes Corporation.

Two incidents provide fascinating glimpses of the historical context of our story. One is from the time of Percy's American sojourn; he told of a day when he was in the city of New York and saw a large crowd of people making for the dock area. It transpired that the survivors of the *Titanic* disaster were being brought to shore. The other is the fact that Percy was 28 years old when the Wright brothers first flew; and that he lived long enough to sit up one night with his son Harry to watch television coverage of Neil Armstrong setting foot on the moon!

After a brief time in Scotland, in 1913 Percy sailed again for South Africa. A fellow-passenger on the ship was Miss Isabel ('Bella') Watt who had spent some months at St Colm's Missionary College in Edinburgh and was on her way to take up a teaching position in Emgwali Girls' School. It was supported by a body with the fulsome title of "The Ladies' Kaffrarian Mission in Connection with the United Free Church for Promoting Female Education in Kaffraria". Bella was born in Crovie, Banffshire in February 1888 and had taught in schools at Badenscoth, New Byth and Spey Bay. Six months after landing, Percy wrote to Isabel; it was the start of a lengthy and increasingly frequent correspondence, the outcome of which was their eventual engagement to be married.

Bella taught at Emgwali from 1913 until the end of 1917. She and Percy were both due home leave, but the First World War intervened and it was decided that Bella, rather than beginning another term with the Free Church Mission, should move upcountry to Nyasaland for the wedding, which took place on 6th February 1918 at Blantyre Church.

"Move up-country to Nyasaland" sounds simple enough when we read the phrase today. In late 1917 it was a different matter. The yellowing pages of Bella's journal tell of an arduous journey by wagon, train and steamer. Writing from somewhere "on the Zambesi" on 27th January that year, Bella's hand-written account says:

> "Where am I to begin this tale? It seems ages since I began the journey (on 15th December) – Emgwali to Dohne by ox wagon, Dohne to East London by goods train"

Christmas came and went, mentioned only as "a quiet but happy Christmas and Boxing Day".

The entry for 15th January gives a sample of the journal:

> "Wakened near Bulawayo. Went and had breakfast at the Grand Hotel. Then went shopping with Mrs Pearson. Very trusting people in B. – gave us credit. I got a silver clock – Frank's present – wish I had time to get Joe's too. Left Bulawayo at 12.15 and sorry to leave my trav. comps. Had a coupe to myself and glad to have room to move at my own sweet will. Country beginning to be more interesting, more like one's idea of Rhodesia – hills & boulders & trees & lovely skies at sunset"

Ten days later –

> "Arrived Chinde at one. Discovered by Mr Fullarton – carried ashore by 2 natives – on shoulder and taken to A.L.C. Hotel. (What a place. The only decent thing about it is that visitors are earnestly requested not to give gratuities to servants! Sensible folk, A.L.C.!)"

Several references are made to bothersome mosquitoes, although Bella seems only to have suffered a degree of itchiness while others succumbed to fever. On 1st February they arrived at Blantyre amid torrents of rain. She records:

> "There was 'himself' – looking so fearfully thin. No empty compartments, but we didn't care. Capt. Wood provided motorcars and got us here – the Rookery. Mrs Selkirk very kind. After tea we went and met the Macdonalds. She's jolly. Then He came back to dinner. Thought they would never clear out, but they did and then we didn't talk business".

And then –

"Wednesday 6th Feb. Our wedding day, and what a day of rain – torrents all the time, going to church and in church and coming back. A good many of the Mandala crowd were there in spite of the rain, but I wish they hadn't thrown red rose leaves in the wet. They stain. I wasn't nervous. It was all very sweet. So ended Isabel Watt; and now comes the luncheon – very nice and very proper."

After listing the small number of people present, fewer than a dozen, she wrote:

"Glad there wasn't a fuss. The cake was cut and a hurried change and we left by motor for Zomba at two. Arrived at four. A cold welcome and all very disappointing – but not Henry – he's always a dear."

The new Mr and Mrs Mantell settled first in Ekwendeni.

In 1919, after the end of the War, the opportunity finally came for home leave and the newlyweds were at last able to travel to Britain to meet their in-laws.

On their return to Africa, they settled in Kasama, Northern Rhodesia and, in due time, looked forward to the birth of their first baby. On 15th October 1921, Bella gave birth to Ruth but tragedy followed when Bella contracted septicaemia and, two weeks later, passed away.

In the weeks and months that followed, various people helped Percy to look after the new baby in Rhodesia, until his next leave in 1924, when he brought her back to be cared for by her family in Macduff.

Percy left every fourth year for his home country. During these periods at home he would meet, among others, Miss Barbara Ann Lyall of Carny Street, Macduff, another school teacher who also happened to be a cousin of Bella's. Bannie (as Barbara Ann was affectionately known throughout her life) taught first in Bracoden School, Gardenstown and then at Balhousie Boys' School, Perth; she loved to tell of one former pupil who said of her, "She told me English!"

The two families, the Watts and the Lyalls, were very friendly; Bannie would sometimes advise on young Ruth's education, and so it posed no great upset to Ruth when a friendship developed between her father and the schoolteacher.

The friendship progressed and Percy and Bannie were married on 12th March 1937 in the then Doune Church. The Aberdeen *Press & Journal* reported that the bride:

"Chose a gown of parchment satin, cut on simple classical lines with a skirt forming a train, she wore a net veil and a coronet of orange blossoms and carried a bouquet of deep cream roses".

The couple settled in Zambia, where three children were born to them. Harry was born at Lusaka in 1939, Elizabeth at Kasama (where Ruth also had been born) in 1941, and Helen at Abercorn in 1944.

During the Second World War, travel was again curtailed and it was in September 1946 that Percy came back to Scotland by sea, followed later by Bannie and the children. Percy had to return to Zambia after four months, but it was decided that Bannie and the children should remain so that Harry and Elizabeth could benefit by a complete year in Macduff Infant School.

When they returned to Zambia, Bannie home-schooled the children. She was asked to organise a proper school in Abercorn for the children of expatriates. It was in that school, which grew to have about 20 pupils, that Elizabeth started her formal education. Ruth, by this time herself a teacher, was given leave of absence from her school in Aberdeen to spend ten months at Abercorn, beginning in December 1950; this gave her the opportunity of getting to know her family better, also the country in which she had been born.

In 1951 Percy retired. He had initially signed up for one period of service with the African Lakes Company, but finally clocked up 45 years' service.

The family sailed home on the M.V. Llangibby Castle of the Union Castle Line; Bannie wrote a letter, headed, "Mediterranean Sea, Sunday 9.9.51". She wrote,

> "The children spend most of their time swimming and Percy reads most of the time. He is looking very much better of the rest".

She also referred to Harry and Elizabeth winning prizes in the ship's sports, and of looking forward to their arrival at Tilbury on 12th or 13th (September). They planned to spend a few days in London "before coming north. I am anxious now to get the children to school"

Elizabeth was enrolled at Macduff Primary School and later Banff Academy. Bannie was a visiting teacher of music and Banff Academy was one of the schools in which she taught. Bannie was known as a musician: she was a Licentiate of the Royal Academy of Music, a singer, pianist, organist and instructor; she also organised a ladies' choir to which Percy gave the nickname, "Bannie's Nightingales".

Elizabeth was apparently not a natural scholar and she did not particularly enjoy her school years. Of a sensitive nature herself, she did not flourish under a rather heavy-handed teacher; she was even told that her education didn't matter very much because she wanted only to be a nurse!

She was keen on sport, however, and a fellow-pupil of those days, Monica Ogg (then Monica Wilson of Gellyhill), remembers sharing Elizabeth's passion for hockey –

> "She in a defensive role, myself as centre forward awaiting the pass to attack the goal, especially if Buckie High School were the opponents! The clear recollection I have is of us both running for the bus home, red-faced, dressing on the move, laden with school-bag, boots and hockey sticks, all the way from Duff House grounds along Low Street to the Plainstones".

Elizabeth Mantell with her Hockey teem

Such was their friendship that Monica invited Elizabeth to be a bridesmaid at her wedding in King's College Chapel, Aberdeen in July 1965. Remarkably, Elizabeth was on duty at Foresterhill to deliver the third Ogg daughter, Ailsa.

> "Elizabeth honoured us by agreeing to be Ailsa's godmother, a duty she took most seriously, and until her untimely death Ailsa adored her godmother's thoughtfulness and kindness".

Interestingly, after Elizabeth's death, the mother of a classmate remarked to Ruth that Elizabeth was the only girl in their particular group who had realised her ambition, which had always been to go back to Africa to nurse the babies. Elizabeth's sister, Helen, remembers the fancy-dress parties they attended as children, when Elizabeth would *always* go as a nurse.

As we have heard, the illustration in her memorial window aptly depicts Elizabeth, in her nursing uniform, holding an African baby. It was no doubt this commitment that led her to turn her back on thoughts of romantic relationships; she was committed to Christian service in Malawi.

Elizabeth looked back with pleasure on her days as a member of the 1st Macduff Girl Guides, when Miss Jess Morrison was the Guider. Activities included summer camps; she was very pleased to gain the status of Queen's Guide, also to be a Scottish Guide at the Guides World Camp at Windsor in 1957.

Another Guide of that time, Kathleen Reid, was her Patrol Leader in the Thistle Patrol and tells of Elizabeth's special love of the outdoor part of guiding, including hiking and camping. Many years later Elizabeth told her former Patrol Leader that her guiding experience had helped with her work in Malawi:

> "Things like fire-lighting and cooking on an open fire (and coping with latrines!) Sometimes came in very handy when she was out in the villages".

Another friend from these Guiding days was Joan Waldron, to whom I am very grateful for much information about Elizabeth's nursing training. The two first met at joint camps held by the Turriff and Macduff Companies. This was the start of another long friendship, later to be kept up in Central Africa. Joan's husband, Martin, worked in Lusaka in the Auditor General's office, as part of British Overseas Aid. During their six years there, Joan worked in the Maternity Department of the University Teaching Hospital. Both Joan and Kathleen spoke fondly of a time spent together in 1976 when Kathleen and Elizabeth, en route for Malawi, stopped in Zambia. The two Waldron children loved their Auntie Liz. Young David treasured a kitten he called "Minty", a name which had nothing to do with its smell but which was the result of an occasion when he tried to get Auntie Liz's attention and was told, "Just a minty" (a north-east Scots diminutive for a 'minute'). David hadn't heard the word before but it lived on as the name of his cuddly friend.

In 1960, at their last camp, Elizabeth and Joan were excited to discover that they were both planning to start nursing at Aberdeen Royal Infirmary on 1st August that year. As already stated, there never was much doubt about which profession Elizabeth would enter; Joan recalls the day when

Elizabeth travelled by bus to Turriff and then Joan's mother drove them to the Elms, a large house in Queen's Gate, Aberdeen, where 40 trainee nurses were to live during their first three months of training. Let Joan tell the story:

> "From Monday to Friday we all walked the mile or two up to the classrooms in Foresterhill Nursing Home for lectures on the basics of nursing – anatomy, physiology, health, nutrition, bandaging, invalid cookery, etc. On Tuesdays, however, we were dressed in our new uniforms, which were starched, too big for us and made us look as if we should know more than we did! We were taken by bus, feeling sick with anxiety, to spend the day in the wards. Elizabeth was in Ward 10F – then a surgical ward. From the very beginning, Elizabeth was a very diligent student, eager to learn, but full of fun too.
>
> "After three months we went to live in the Nurses' Home in Foresterhill and we were often on different shifts – 'split shifts': i.e. 7 – 9 am for everyone, then we might have a morning off from 9 am – 1 pm, or an afternoon from 1 – 5 pm, or an evening off from 5 pm. The day shift finished at 9 pm. We had 1½ days off per week but very few weekends. We usually ended the day with a crowd of us sitting on the bed or floor of someone's room, drinking milky coffee or hot chocolate, happily chatting. In those days we accepted these hours without question, but they did make social life rather difficult. Our training in A.R.I. was exceptional and stood us all in good stead for our future careers."

Church attendance was not always easy with such variable hours, but Elizabeth attended High Holburn sometimes, also a Baptist Church.

In due time, Elizabeth became a State Registered Nurse and followed this with a further year at Queen Charlotte's Maternity Hospital in London where she qualified as a midwife. Elizabeth and Joan arrived at Queen Charlotte's in Hammersmith on 16th December 1963, feeling disappointed at having to leave their families so close to Christmas. However, family members in Romford and Teddington helped the two nurses feel welcome.

"London", according to Joan,

> eg "Was exciting. We were near the Thames and we watched the Boat Race start on television and then ran down to the river to watch them go past! In true Aberdonian fashion (so people say!), they would go along to Wimbledon at about 5 pm and accept tickets offered by people leaving at that time; they saw some wonderful evening matches. During that time they worshipped at St Columba's Church of Scotland in Pont Street and sometimes also at Richmond Baptist Church."

When they were first being shown around the Hospital, they were taken to the Milk Bank; Queen Charlotte's supplied breast milk expressed by mothers in the hospital and local district who had too much milk to supply to mothers who didn't have enough. As Joan recalls:

> "In the Unit all the bottles had "EBM" on them and Elizabeth's face was a picture when she saw her initials (her middle name was Barbara), not knowing at first what they stood for!"

Joan tells of their Second Part Midwifery Training, which lasted for six happy and very busy months. Sometimes midwives who had cars would drive them out on calls, but:

> "Most of the pre- and post-natal visits were done on our bikes, with our black bags on our carriers behind us. Guided by our copies of "A – Z", we cycled through Hammersmith, Chiswick, Shepherds Bush, Acton, etc. Fortunately the traffic wasn't so bad then and we were young and fearless! I do remember that one day Elizabeth lost her way and ended up being shouted at by a lorry driver that she was going up onto the Chiswick flyover – where bikes weren't allowed. She had to turn round and wheel her bike down against the traffic!"

In 1964 Barbara Kwast from the Netherlands was appointed as a teaching district midwife and became a friend of Elizabeth's. Barbara talks about the long hours they worked –

> "I remember that Elizabeth was always very caring and aware when colleagues or situations needed extra support. We soon started to share our concerns during short prayer times when at all possible. Elizabeth had a special love for the Lord and radiated a security which was difficult to describe".

After losing touch for a time, Barbara and Elizabeth met up again in Malawi. Barbara was working for the Netherlands government in Lilongwe and heard that Elizabeth was working at the Mlanje Mission Hospital. Sometimes they would help each other with marking exam papers, and Barbara writes of watching Elizabeth at work –

> "Especially at the under-5s clinics. Elizabeth's dedication and care for these children and their parents were exemplary and taught us so much".

However this is jumping ahead.

Chapter 3
The Missionary

After the completion of her extra year's training, Elizabeth worked for a time in Aberdeen, but she increasingly sensed the call of God, marking her life for missionary service. No doubt her early days in Africa had left their mark in her heart, but her commitment to Africa cannot be explained in such terms alone. She saw her work there as a service given to God in response to the gospel of Christ; it was in 1966, at the age of 25, that she returned to Africa.

The Church of Scotland's Overseas Council was so desperate for nurses at Mlanje in the south of Malawi that they gladly sent her at short notice. It was only during her first furlough that she undertook a term's study at the Church's missionary training college, St. Colm's, in Edinburgh.

A press cutting from 1966 (probably from the Banffshire Journal) reported:

> "The evening service in Doune Church on Sunday was conducted by the Rev Grahame R. Walker. It took the form of a farewell service for Miss E. Mantell, who has accepted a two year appointment as a missionary in Mlanje Hospital, Malawi. The lessons were read by Messrs James R. West and E. A. Porterfield, two members of the Kirk Session. After the service, in the Market Street Hall, a gift was presented to Miss Mantell by the Rev G. R. Walker. Tea was provided by members of the Guild. Solos were rendered by Mrs James West".

The article recorded a request which Elizabeth had made for reading spectacles and, in another cutting (*Evening Express*, 13.4.66), she was quoted as saying:

> "I do two years out there for a start. At the moment I don't know if I'll be staying on longer or not!"

Mlanje is 47 miles South-East of Blantyre; the first hospital had been erected on the site of the original Mlanje Mission (now a tea estate) around 1890. In 1930 the move was made to the present site, which provided 28 beds and a delivery room. Later additions included an outpatients' department, isolation wards and accommodation for midwives and for students. In 1958 two more wards were added, along with an operating theatre. The hospital then had 64 beds, although it often accommodated more than 100 patients at a time!

During Elizabeth's period of service at Mlanje, there were about 150 deliveries every month, with 1500 women being seen at antenatal clinics; 2500-3000 patients were also seen every month at under-5s clinics in the hospital and in district clinics.

This is where Elizabeth worked from 1966 – 1971, serving as a Midwifery Sister, also teaching student nurses. There was little time for formal language study and she learned Chichewa as she taught. Perhaps because of this grass-roots learning, she became fluent in Chichewa and maintained in later years that she was much more at home with the Chichewa of the south than with the Chitumbuka of the north.

An early letter (March 1967) spoke of both success and failure in the work.

> "Take for instance the case of Dyson, the boy of five who came to us fairly ill, but we could find no cause for it. He became thinner and thinner, refusing to eat and losing weight and losing all desire to live, and finally he died. Yet again we had the case of Abibi, two years old and weighing 15 pounds, who came in with kwashiorkor, which is malnutrition plus a severe lack of vitamins, which causes open sores all over the body. A month later he was discharged weighing 18 pounds and looking a different child. We thank God for being able to help at least some of these children"

In the same letter she wrote of the staff's involvement in other areas. Her colleague, Helen Scott, conducted a Sunday School teachers' class; Norma Burnett was leading the local Girls' Brigade; while Elizabeth herself was helping Mrs Rennie, the minister's wife, with the local "Mvano" (Woman's Guild) sewing class;

> "We teach the women to both sew and knit and they get great pleasure in seeing what they can turn out. It may be anything from a simple hem by the older women to a dress by the younger girls, but at least it is their own work"

During these early years Elizabeth expressed the love for people that was an integral part of her whole life. She would have been embarrassed by many of the tributes paid to her after she died, but it is true that she maintained a steady love for people and was motivated by that care and concern. We remember visiting her once in her terminal illness and finding her in some discomfort. She folded her arms against her abdomen in an attempt to lessen the pain but nevertheless, in the midst of it all, came out with: "I just wish I was out there (in Malawi) with my girls". That care and concern characterized her life. Her service was not simply that of a nurse who happened to be working in a hospital outside Britain; her service was the service of one who saw it in terms of the Lord's words in Matthew 25:35:

> "I was hungry and you gave me something to eat, I was thirsty and you gave me something to drink, I was a stranger and you invited me in, I needed clothes and you clothed me, I was sick and you looked after me..."

That care for others did not stop at the hospital gates. Her great desire was for the best for 'her girls' and she carried out many acts of kindness by stealth. Among those who frequented the khonde (veranda) outside Elizabeth's house in Ekwendeni were several who were being supported in different ways by her. We found it difficult to get much information about this, as Elizabeth was not keen to talk about it, but we were aware that she was supporting various people in very practical, including monetary ways.

During a visit to Ekwendeni in 1991, Joan Waldron remarked on how peaceful it was in Elizabeth's house. Elizabeth smiled and said, "Not always". But, Joan goes on,

Elizabeth's table with assorted items

"...she had a wonderful way of making us feel so special, our time together so valuable in spite of all the work overload which was on her shoulders all the time. She entertained so well – always books to look at, tapes to listen to, jigsaws on the table in the corner, fruit and macadamia nuts available, games to play – she introduced me to Rummikub by solar panel light while we stayed by the Lake for a few days near Livingstonia. She baked banana bread in her primitive kitchen at 5 am because it was the only time available before we set off on a trip."

Joan's experience while walking with Elizabeth along the shores of Lake Malawi one day expresses much about Elizabeth's inner attitude.

"I was admiring her for all the work she did, how she served the Lord in such a sacrificial way, but she didn't see it that way at all, saying that the Lord uses all of us wherever we are and that my work for Him here in my own community was just as important."

But despite such denials, Joan's estimation would be seconded by many when she writes, "But she really was a remarkable person." She goes on to write about Elizabeth's love for people:

"Her students were all special to her. She cared for them in a motherly way — aware of their being far from home, with time on their hands in the evenings. So she ran sewing classes by candlelight before the hospital had electricity, she would show them videos (this was before Malawi had television), she would take them to the Lake for a picnic and swimming, with coffee in a hotel in Mzuzu on the way."

Nor was this practical help confined to 'her' girls. Another of Elizabeth's visitors, Margaret Sinclair, records as her most vivid memory of Elizabeth a simple incident, which occurred on someone else's khonde.

"A young woman passed, head bowed against the wind and the rain, carrying a baby and holding a small child's hand. The rains had well and truly come and we were sitting shivering on the khonde, but Elizabeth got up and ran after the young woman and gave her the cardigan she was wearing, explaining when she re-joined us that this young woman attended one of their clinics and her man was working far away. I felt it was truly scriptural – even if she no doubt had other cardigans at home".

Elizabeth was also aware of the teamwork that is involved in mission and, during the later period she spent at home looking after her mother, she wrote in 1975 for the (then) Doune Church's quarterly magazine about the importance of home support for those in the field. The article was entitled, *Prayer and Blue Letters*. Elizabeth wrote:

"How can we pray more thoughtfully for the work at Mlanje Missionary Hospital, with which we have been associated as a congregation for some years now? Dr John Phillips, our prayer partner, is medical superintendent – and his task is no light one. We at home can make it lighter by prayer, with as much information and understanding as possible."

She wrote about some of the issues facing the hospital then: the construction of new buildings and the difficulty of keeping "the young up-and-coming nurse once she has trained".

She went on:

"These are but a few of the problems – but God sees the tasks and his strength is all-sufficient. Remember that God works through us at home too, but those 'in the field' must know that we are thinking of them. What better way than through a few lines in a blue airmail? There is always great excitement when blue letters arrive – telling of home happenings and showing that someone is remembering. So why not let the 'blue' be from you – letting Dr Phillips know that our thoughts and prayers are with him in the work that he is doing for Christ and His kingdom?"

Elizabeth was herself a prolific letter-writer, and reference will be made later to some of her letters from Malawi. She greatly appreciated letters from home, and was reluctant to accept any assurances that people would understand if they didn't receive a reply to every letter.

And if blue letters were important, so was prayer. Her letters are permeated with prayer: gratitude for prayer, encouragements to prayer, specific requests for prayer. Her official letters usually listed specific subjects requiring prayer at the time when she was writing; she would also frequently testify to the power of prayer.

In her last Partner Plan letter, in which she informed people of her retirement on health grounds, she looked back and wrote,

"The main thing I have been aware of is the wonderful support a group of praying people can give. How wonderful to belong to that fellowship. We were given strength, hope and healing and these lines from Romans 8 v 37 have been very real: 'In all things we are more than conquerors through Him who loved us'."

This emphasis on prayer is borne out in an account she gave of a time of difficulty in early 1994 in Ekwendeni. She wrote in her Partner Plan letter:

"We never know what is ahead of us but it is a comfort to know that we are never alone. We have been so aware of the Lord's protection and care and of the tremendous support in prayer we have had."

And what she wrote at the end of her life was expressed at that time also:

"To belong to such a family of caring and praying people has been a privilege to experience".

One evening, while she and some colleagues were sitting listening to a tape, thieves broke into her bedroom.

"I went out to make a phone call, disturbed them at their game and foolishly asked one what he thought he was doing. He obviously did not like to be asked a question like this and drew something out of his jacket and advanced. It did not take me long to retreat. We all went into the bedroom only to see a second person climbing out of the window. The only thing they had taken was a small brief case of written and addressed Christmas cards which a friend, Francis Sutcliffe, had spent the week writing. We prayed that the boys would take pity and post the cards when they found out the contents of the case. Who knows?"

It was the following night that another colleague, Elma, was abducted at knifepoint. A student heard her scream and raised the alarm. Elizabeth remarked on the fact that, within minutes, people from all over the station had rallied round to assist in the search and that, in less than an hour, people all over the world were praying for her.

"A prayer vigil was started here and we prayed that the Lord would just bind the evil one and He did. Four hours later Elma escaped and returned to us."

In the midst of such drama and turmoil, she recounted:

"We were so aware of the power of prayer and of God's presence, and so thankful to see her safe return". She asked for continuing prayer for Elma and concluded, "On behalf of all the people here I would like to say thank you for your support through prayer and for becoming a closer part of the family here that night."

Elizabeth's time in Mlanje, however, was to be shorter than she had anticipated. After her father's death in 1971, it was realized that her mother was increasingly forgetful. Elizabeth came home and when she saw that her mother was in need of her help, she resigned her position in order to return to Macduff.

There were people who thought it unlikely that Elizabeth would ever return to Malawi after a period that turned out to last ten years; they didn't realise that you might take Elizabeth out of Africa, but you couldn't take Africa out of Elizabeth.

Chapter 4
The Daughter

When she returned from Malawi in 1971, Elizabeth had no idea of what the future held. It would be ten years before her mother's death, when she would again be in a position to consider her future.

She cared lovingly for her mother during that period as Bannie, with the passing of the years, became increasingly forgetful and then gradually more frail. She died in October 1980 at the age of 80.

During this period at home, Elizabeth worked as a District Nurse in Macduff, Banff and the surrounding area and also undertook some further study. She qualified as a Clinical Tutor in Midwifery and gained a community nursing qualification.

For us in the Manse, Elizabeth was always a welcome visitor (not to mention baby-sitter) and valued friend. One of our children didn't always agree with that assessment; when Andrew was only a few weeks old, he was seriously ill with bronchitis. More than a year later, when he had a chest infection, he was subjected to a course of injections, administered by ladies in nursing uniform. Elizabeth was attached to another medical practice so was often in uniform when she dropped in. It was some time before Andrew accepted that Elizabeth hadn't come to do any nasty things to him with needles, and gradually came to trust her!

During these years at home, Elizabeth was approached by the Kirk Session about ordination to the eldership; after much thought and prayer, she agreed to take on that leadership role. She visited faithfully in her district and sought to care for her flock. She also served for a year as a representative elder in Buchan Presbytery.

She also devoted much time to youth work. At the time we had moved our teens' Bible Class to a Monday evening, with a teaching time and then a time for games and other activities of a more social nature, Elizabeth gave of her time and energy to leadership within this group.

For some time she wrote reports for the church magazine to keep the congregation aware of what was happening. In the June 1976 issue, she wrote:

"Many of the young people who attended this session's meetings had no church connection; we did not know if some who came had come to distract the others or if they genuinely were seeking – but we pray that they met with a challenge which they will one day accept. This is what the church is for – to show those who seek the way to Jesus".

Later, in June 1981, she wrote,

"We again ask for the congregation's continued prayers for the young folk of our church, that they may have a grounding and knowledge of the Word that will be with them all their lives".

Another, perhaps surprising, aspect of that time is that it seemed to help Elizabeth herself to gain confidence in public speaking. Once she was back to Malawi, and when it transpired that one of the main aspects of her work was to teach others, she looked back on that time at home as a learning experience. Soon after returning, she wrote,

"I am now very glad of the time spent with the Bible Class on a Friday night (it had changed from Monday) – because through it I have not found it so difficult to stand up in front of a class and teach as I might have done if I had not done anything like that. The Lord does indeed know what is before us and in His own way prepares us for everything".

However, she did not regard herself as a public speaker; in fact, during later deputation visits to the various churches with which she was linked particularly in the Presbyteries of Buchan and Dunoon, she dreaded the thought of having to speak. She did enjoy her contacts with many people in many places, but the thought of getting up on a platform or in a pulpit was another matter!

One of the few remains of that public work is a handwritten script for an address to children. It is included here as a sample of Elizabeth's public speaking work.

"Let me tell you about two little girls who came to our hospital in Africa. Their names were Hilda and Balandiwo. When Hilda was very small, her Mummy died and her Daddy thought as there was no-one in the village to look after her, she would die, so he brought her to our hospital and asked us if we would look after her till she was older. Now we had a lot of other babies to look after, so we asked her daddy if there was anyone he could think of in his family that would be able to come and help us look after Hilda. He thought for a little and then said that the only one he could think of was Hilda's sister, Balandiwo. But Balandiwo was only 8 years old.

"Balandiwo came along and although she was only 8 years old, she was taught how to feed, wash and dress Hilda, and she loved her very much.

"As Balandiwo had never been to school (her Daddy did not have enough money to send her) she learned to read and write, although she did not really like doing this very much. She preferred to be with her little sister all the time.

"She did like going to Sunday School and every Sunday she would tie Hilda to her back with a long cloth (this is how they carry babies in Africa) and off she would go and join the other children, hearing stories about Jesus, how He loves us all, and that He wants us to love everyone,

"She knew she was not good at writing and reading, but she was happy as she knew she was good at looking after Hilda, just as Jesus would want her to do. She knew she was not too young to do something to please Jesus. They have both now gone back to the village and Hilda is growing into a nice strong girl."

Even though Elizabeth did not relish the thought of giving talks and sermons, those who heard her various addresses were impressed, not only with what she said but by the sincerity and obvious commitment of her life. They could see that she was, as one listener put it, one who had given her all. He, without any doubt, had the hymn, "When I survey the wondrous cross" in mind, for it talks about Christ's 'love so amazing' demanding our souls, our lives, our all. Whether at home or away, Elizabeth gave her all in the service of the Lord and of other people.

Anyone who didn't know her well would have been surprised to hear her occasionally refer to someone as an "impudent baggage"! It was only years later that I discovered the phrase in George Bernard Shaw's play, *Saint Joan*. Spoken by Elizabeth, it might sometimes hold a hint of impatience, especially when the person so designated did not live up to her high standards, but the expression would often be accompanied by a twinkle in her eye.

During that period at home, Elizabeth also enjoyed being part of the church family at home. She had an appetite for God's Word; she was always eager to learn more and she took part in as many meetings as possible.

On departure from Macduff, a congregational farewell social was held after her valedictory service, when various presentations were made to her. It was not an occasion to which she had looked forward, such was her dread of publicity, but it proved to be one of fellowship, one on which she later looked back with pleasure and gratitude.

Chapter 5
The Nurse

After the death of her mother, when many people expected her to settle down to life on her own in Macduff, Elizabeth became convinced of God's call to return to Malawi.

Shortly after Bannie's death a circular for display on church notice boards came from the Church's Board of World Mission. Included was the position of Sister Tutor at Ekwendeni Mission Hospital in Malawi. I remember my wife saying, "Don't put that up; we'll lose Elizabeth"! And we did. Elizabeth's contribution to the life and fellowship of the church here during that period was such that it was difficult to contemplate losing her, but our loss would undoubtedly be Malawi's gain, and it was really no surprise to hear Elizabeth speak of a sense of divine calling to return to Africa.

A valedictory service was held for her on 6th February 1983. The text for the sermon was 2 Corinthians 12:9: "My grace is sufficient for you". This became a key verse for Elizabeth, as has already been noted in connection with the design of her memorial window in Macduff Church. The design, with that text reaching right across it, is intended to convey the message that Elizabeth's life also was shot through with faith, the faith which holds that, even through our weakness and inadequacy - and no one was more aware of that inadequacy than Elizabeth - God's grace can be at work.

At the dedication service for the memorial window, I recalled some words I once heard given by Professor James S. Stewart from an Edinburgh pulpit. He had referred to such people as Eric Liddell, Albert Schweitzer and C.T. Studd in remarking: "What daft things people do for Christ's sake"! To many people, Elizabeth's decision to return to Africa must have seemed daft. She was 41 years old; she had already given service to Africa; she could have held down a good position at home; no one would have criticised her if she had settled into life in Britain. An aunt who, as it happened, passed away before Elizabeth had actually left for Ekwendeni, had actually said to her: "Now that you're over 40, you'll be too old..."

Memorial Window

However, nothing was going to deflect Elizabeth from her avowed intent to be a medical missionary. Two things motivated her. One was her love for

Africa, which had been part of her from the very beginning of her life, and the other was the call of the Lord. She was sure that it was God's will that she should serve in Malawi. She communicated with the World Mission department of the Church of Scotland and was duly assigned to Ekwendeni Hospital in northern Malawi.

So she departed for Malawi once again to take up a position in the maternity department of that 200-bed hospital, which served a primary healthcare area of some 400 square miles and a population of 45,000. Elizabeth would sometimes comment on the contrast in travel over the generations. In 1920 the journey took about two months; Elizabeth flew out overnight. When Robert Laws went to Africa, it would sometimes be ten months before he would receive a reply to letters home; in Elizabeth's time the blue airmails arrived quickly, although parcels were sometimes another matter. She could also use the telephone. Nowadays, of course, the world has shrunk and news items discussed at missionary prayer meetings can be unprecedentedly up-to-date, arriving often as emails that may have been written on the very same day.

Malawi's tourist slogan is "The Warm Heart of Africa", a title amply justified by the happiness of its people and the welcome they extend. A tourist leaflet (published by Lorton Communications) says enticingly:

> "You'll be enthralled by our friendly people and welcomed with smiles and warm greetings. Along Lake Malawi's palm fringed shore the days are long and lazy. Enjoy the water sports or relax on the golden beaches. Our un-spoilt National Parks and game reserves are blessed with a rich diversity of wildlife. Explore these by car or on foot in the company of a game guard – but wherever you go take your camera – you'll want to record all the wonders you'll see here in Malawi, the warm heart of Africa!"

And it's true! Visitors to Malawi find a warm welcome and also a spirit of generosity, which can be challenging when set against the background of the poverty of the people. The nation is one of small-scale farmers, with maize being the main crop. Cattle, goats, pigs and chicken are also reared; the present writer remembers the excitement of visiting a chicken-rearing project in Ekwendeni.

However, the apostle Paul's words about the churches of Macedonia could be applied to many in Malawi who happily share the little that they have. Reserved Britons may sometimes be surprised at the unashamed frankness with which Malawians can ask for help, but such open requests need to be seen against the background of their own willingness to share whatever they have with others. In 2 Corinthians 8:2 (New English Bible) Paul wrote about the way in which the Macedonian Christians had faced their troubles:

> "...yet in all this they have been so exuberantly happy that from the depths of their poverty they have shown themselves lavishly open-handed"

The same could be said of so many Malawians.

Malawi is a land-locked country of 118,000 square km, 20% of which is taken up by Lake Malawi, the third largest lake in Africa. It became a British colony, the "Central African Protectorate" in 1891 and, in 1907, was given the name Nyasaland. It gained independence in 1964. Its main export crops are cotton, tea, tobacco and groundnuts; both maize and fishing are very important parts of the country's economy.

Sadly, it remains one of the world's poorest countries. In 2005, according to an article in *The Healing Hand* (the magazine of Emmanuel Healthcare; Volume 63, Number 2), a Household Survey conducted by the Malawian National Statistical Office uncovered some striking facts about the state of the nation. Some of the statistics tell the story:

- The survey defined as "poor" those whose consumption was less than 16,165 Malawian Kwacha per annum, (approximately £61 sterling) and as "ultra poor" those consuming less than 10,029 MK per annum (approximately £38). According to that formula, 6.4 million of Malawi's population of 12 million were classed as "poor" - i.e. 52% - including 2.7 million (22%) as "ultra poor". This represents a rise of 1.1 million "poor" people over a period of eight years.

- The rural population still lives in mud houses with thatched roofs; 72% live in such homes.

- 2% have a water tap in their homes, with only a further 18% having access to a communal stand-pipe.

- In rural areas, 1.9% have access to electric light, compared to 5.6% of the total population, There is a dependence on wood for cooking purposes and this has consequences in terms of deforestation.

- 56% of people felt that they had inadequate food, 72% inadequate clothes and 60% inadequate healthcare. Compared to eight years ago, only 19% of the "poor" felt that they were better off; 34% thought there was no change and 47% felt they were worse off.

As for healthcare, Malawi has 27 district hospitals and 11 CHAM hospitals (Christian Health Association of Malawi). All district hospitals, according to an NHS Bulletin issued by the Scottish Executive Health Department in May 2006, are severely understaffed with an average of one nurse per ward. Per 100,000 of population, Malawi has 1.1 doctors and 25.5 nurses; this compares poorly with other African countries.

Other statistics relative to health care in Malawi can be tabulated as follows (with some comparative figures for the UK):

	Malawi	UK
Population	12.1 million	60.4 million
Birth rate per 1000 population	44.7	10.78
Life expectancy	38	78.45
Death rate per 1000 population	22.6	10.18
Infant mortality per 1000 live births	104	5.14
Maternal mortality per 100,000 live births	1120	
Attendance at birth by trained staff	55%	
Fertility (children born per woman)	6.3	1.66
Population aged 15 or younger	46%	
Under-5 chronic malnourishment	49%	
HIV/AIDS prevalence rate	14.20%	0.20%
HIV/AIDS – people living with	1 million	51,000
HIV/AIDS – deaths annually	84,000	500

(some additional information from: "USA, The World Factbook 2005")

Before returning to Elizabeth's work at Ekwendeni, it may be of interest to read the description given of the hospital by the then Chief Executive of Emmanuel Healthcare, Robin Arnott, who visited the hospital in May/June 2005:

> "A flagship hospital in the north of Malawi, Ekwendeni has expanded considerably in the last two years and the new Primary Healthcare Department (PHC) building is now open and functioning. The new Outpatients Department, which was opened and dedicated last year, has settled down well and has improved the way in which patients are treated.

> "With its new premises, PHC is now regarded as a 'Centre of Excellence' and Kistone Mhango, the Director, is justifiably proud of what it is achieving, from maternal and child health care at 14 outreach clinics, through malaria control programmes and Savings and Credit schemes to water and sanitation and food security.
>
> "Esther Lupafya, the HIV and AIDS Coordinator, told us how they had spent the £10,000 we had given them for orphan care. 'We paid some secondary school fees, bought food and provided fertilizer and bought pigs and chickens. Villagers will breed the animals, sell the piglets or eggs and chickens to generate income and use the animals as food to provide an enhanced diet, particularly for AIDS patients on anti-retroviral drugs. It is a self-sustaining Programme'
>
> "A visit to an ante-natal outreach clinic was an interesting way to spend a morning. Student nurses were hard at work, weighing patients, taking blood pressure and patient histories. They were supplementing the regular nurses, and the Medical Assistants, who were carrying out immunizations, checks for malnutrition and supplying nutritional supplements"

My wife and I visited such an outreach clinic in August 1996 and found it a moving experience. Women with children tied to their backs, had walked for miles to get to the clinic. A few brought produce from their gardens to sell; these goods were often bought by hospital staff for the hospital. It was wonderful to see people following Jesus in caring for the sick in a very practical way.

So, Elizabeth returned to Malawi in 1983. One of her early letters to Joan Waldron (16.3.83) explains that she was required to undergo an orientation period before taking up the work at Ekwendeni.

> "This week I am at St. John's Hospital, Mzuzu (our nearest town – about fifteen miles from Ekwendeni). It is not a very big place, but it has one of the hospitals that are recognized as places for orientation. All people who come into the country to work have to go for a month's orientation at a hospital different from their own. However, I'm only to be a fortnight – but am pleased at the opportunity to get back into doing breeches and twins and sections and vacuums once again. It is a Catholic hospital and most of the sisters are southern Irish and very kind and helpful indeed"

After she had settled in Ekwendeni, one of Elizabeth's first letters sought to introduce her correspondents to the village and the mission station. On 16th May of that year she wrote,

"For those of you who know little of this area, Ekwendeni, geographically termed a 'Trading Centre', is in the Northern Region of Malawi. Our nearest town is Mzuzu, 15 miles away and we can reach it in about 20 minutes on the lovely new tar road. Before this was opened the journey took about 45 minutes by the old dirt road. We do our main shopping in Mzuzu, but can buy fruit and some vegetables at the local market. The mission is the main part of Ekwendeni and consists of the Church and the station offices, the hospital, the Girls' Secondary School, the College of Commerce, a Blind School, the Primary School, Nursery School, Correspondence School, Carpentry School and Lay Training Centre. The Mission was first established at the beginning of the century when the church was built. It is a very imposing building, which is the central point of the mission – and reminds us of how we must keep God central in all our thought".

This concept of the Church in the centre is a powerful illustration of the way in which all aspects of the station focus around the worship and service of God. The centrality of the church is a powerful message in itself. Elizabeth also saw it as a symbol of the centrality of Christian faith, commitment and service in her own life.

Elizabeth's letter goes on to describe the hospital itself.

"This present building was opened in 1958. The buildings are fairly old now and in need of a good deal of repair. They consist of a female ward and male ward, TB ward, laboratory, dental room, theatre, maternity ward with ante-natal and a premature baby ward. The Nurses' Hostel and class rooms are a little way from the main hospital buildings, but they are up to date and a pleasure to work in. We train Enrolled Nurses"

A hospital, however, is not merely a set of buildings. A letter written in March 1995 gives an insight into the sheer busyness of the hospital. Elizabeth wrote:

"The children's ward is absolutely full these days. Children with malaria, anemia and malnutrition. One night last week I went into the ward at night to give out some more blankets as there had been so many admissions there were not enough mats or blankets or sheets to cope with the numbers coming in. There were no fewer than six children on the intensive-care bed; each had a drip up of either fluid or blood and as I looked around the ward there was only space to walk up the middle".

Aids, of course, had become a major issue in Malawi, as in many countries. Elizabeth's letter of February 1992 referred to one lady who had lost a daughter and grandchild through Aids.

"The problem is getting worse. More and more children are being orphaned because of Aids. One man is looking after no fewer than 16 children – his own and those of his dead brother. Many grandparents are being left to care for their grandchildren. What does the future mean for them? Where do they get enough to feed all these mouths, apart from anything else? Those who live within reach of a hospital are able to get supplies of Soya flour from the hospital factory. This helps a little but there is much more that we will have to do."

Elizabeth's own principal area of work was in antenatal and maternity care and the training of future midwives. It was a very demanding job and she was constantly busy. The last paragraph of a letter written on 16th May 1983 expressed her thanks for people's letters and prayers which, she said, had meant so much to her in her settling-in period.

"Oh, it all seemed so much at the beginning, but how much help I got and still get from these verses given to me at my Valedictory Service: 'My grace is sufficient for you'. I am feeling more settled now, although I am still not into a house of my own – the one I'm going into is being renovated at the moment. I have been sharing with Elizabeth Campbell who is Headmistress of the Girls' Secondary School. It has been good to be able to share while getting to know people before moving in to a house of my own, and I give much thanks for that. I have found settling in to the classroom difficult and it is hard work keeping on top of everything every day, but I have been very aware of people's prayers in this matter and give thanks for that too".

A speaker at the 1911 General Assembly of the United Free Church said of Dr Laws,

"I venture to believe that Dr Laws never thinks a thought by day or dreams a dream by night which is not related to the redemption of Africa" (quoted by H. McIntosh, p.172).

Much the same could be said of Elizabeth. Her great and motivating desire was to see others coming to a living faith in the Redeemer. Her desire was that, in everything, Christ might have the pre-eminence (Colossians 1:18); her every activity was devoted to His service and to the good of those among whom she lived and worked.

Elizabeth once wrote about visiting an old lady whom she found sitting quietly in front of her house.

"She had had a stroke some years ago and is not able to speak, but she understands all that is being said. We spoke of the Lord and things concerning Him, and her face just lit up at the mention of Jesus.

> Although she could not speak I felt that we had shared something of His love for us all."

This same concern was expressed in a letter that referred to an evangelistic rally, which was held in August 1983. A team from Scotland under the leadership of the late Captain Stephen Anderson was conducting the mission and people came from all over northern Malawi. She told of many people giving their lives to Christ or coming to a time of recommitment, and wrote:

> "Please pray for these young folk of the north as they return to their congregations – that their counsellors would not lose touch with them and that they would get real feeding and nourishment in the Word, so that their faith would continue to grow".

Elizabeth rejoiced in the appointment in 1986 of a hospital evangelist, Mr Kamanga, whose role was to talk to patients and their relatives and encourage them at a time of spiritual need. Shortly after his appointment, she wrote:

> "Already the Lord has used him in bringing people who have been patients to knowledge of the Lord's saving grace".

As for Elizabeth herself, John Knowles, who served as a doctor at Ekwendeni, has described her as "a wonderful colleague to have". His letters continue:

> "We think ourselves most blessed to have worked for so many years with her. Always kind, polite, caring, loving, thoughtful, and tireless in carrying out her assignment"

They remember her being especially fond of the children:

> "Providing them with drawing materials on the khonde and then juice and biscuits as she chatted with them - they knew that she loved each one"

As these recollections confirm: "She seemed altogether at home in Africa".

Chapter 6
The Tutor

Two months after her valedictory service, Elizabeth wrote about listening again to the audio-tape of the service -

> "...and giving thanks for the words of the text He gave to me. How much I have needed this assurance of His grace being sufficient for me and that it IS – not 'was' or 'will be'. I have often questioned why He has put me here because there seem to be so many things that I am having to do that I never thought I was capable of and yet have to do because there is nobody else to do them and because they have to be done in the course of teaching and caring for the students."

She went on to speak of a growing realization that, although she had in earlier years seen her work more as dealing with patients, now it was to be more with the training of student nurses. She threw herself into her work as a Midwifery Tutor and many would regard this training of others as Elizabeth's most significant contribution to healthcare in Malawi.

She described the two-year course undertaken by the student nurses: an emphasis in the first year on anatomy, physiology and health and hygiene, together with other "odds and ends" of subjects, which she hadn't covered since her own general training which, as she remarked, "wasn't yesterday"! The second year placed more emphasis on midwifery; Elizabeth confessed that she sometimes had to work hard to keep one step ahead of the class. It was sometimes hard going, hard enough for her to admit:

> "Many is the day that I thought I would just come home but for that text. His grace **IS** sufficient for me."

Six weeks later (28th May 1983) she wrote about a few weeks of particular busyness. She had been the only sister on duty and was perhaps feeling it hard to live up to her own high expectations:

> "As I spend most of my time in the classroom the girls are just not getting the proper supervision in the wards. With having to go into the wards more, it means a lot of my office-work has to be left and done after hours – once all the lectures are ready for the next day, so very often it is late before I can get to bed"

Some nights, she said, she hadn't been sleeping very well –

> "Simply because there seem to be so many things to cope with – and last weekend I was sick too."

Busyness and tiredness feature often in Elizabeth's letters, as in a 1985 letter when she spoke of having had to dismiss her nurses' class at 3 pm as she was so tired that she could hardly stand. Nonetheless, she would also write:

> "Despite this, I find life exciting and interesting and I know the Lord never gives us more than we can cope with; and that keeps me going."

A correspondent had asked about a typical day. "Well", Elizabeth replied,

> "Mine is slightly different from the others because I am in the classroom all the time. I start at 7.30 am and have office work to do until 9 am when the girls come into class. Each group has a study day and this means they come in from 9 am – 4 pm. So I have them all day. Each group is at a different stage, so this means covering all subjects – anatomy, physiology, nursing, pharmacology, nutrition, public health, midwifery, microbiology, etc, etc. – and because so many of these subjects I have not done since P.T.S. it means a lot of preparation the night before! Sometimes it is past midnight before I'm finished and then up early the next day, so there has been little time for anything else. I have been very tired – but I am enjoying the challenge and it is interesting. It is usually about 5.30 pm, before I get up to the house. I have to try and keep an eye on what is doing in the hospital too – but find that there is only so much I can do!"

This work of training nurses is undoubtedly a major part of Elizabeth's legacy to Malawi. As a nursing sister she could have helped - and did help - many people but, through her training of many other nurses, she was able to help so many more. It would be impossible to compute the number of people helped by "Liz's girls". Dr John Dorward has written of how, by the time she had to leave Malawi in 1996, seriously ill:

> "She left a thriving Nurses' Training School that had been developed from the previous Midwifery School as a result of her hard work and determination"

A Partner Plan Letter of March 1991 shared two pieces of good news. One was that the threat of the cessation of government grants, which might have threatened the continuance of the hospital, had been lifted. The other was:

> "We have been given the go-ahead for the commencement of the General Training School. The first intake will be in October. Please pray that the girls who will be chosen will be the right ones who will make

good nurses. It is a demanding training and much is demanded of them once they are qualified. One of our prayers is that not only will the girls be well trained in nursing and midwifery but that they will also have a strong Christian commitment"

Dr Dorward wrote of Elizabeth's vision of a balanced, integrated nursing and midwifery course:

"She planned, worked and prayed through the development of a school that would teach high quality, appropriate nursing and midwifery. Liz's work has produced benefit not only to her students and the many scattered institutions in which they work throughout Malawi, but also to the countless Malawians who are now nursed and cared for by 'Liz's girls'. Team working with Dr John Knowles, Matron Mrs Kapunda and hostel manager Mama NyaKumwonga kept the school integrated in the hospital as a whole and ensured the students felt part of the larger hospital team"

Elizabeth set high standards for herself and for others. Stella Eusebio describes her as

"A good judge of character (who) was not afraid to let members of staff know if she thought that they were being lazy or not working at the level of which they were capable"

Writing at the time of the threatened strike by nurses (which is mentioned below), she would write with candour to Ruth:

"I could knock their blocks off, especially as they are the best paid staff in the country, never mind C.H.A.M. (Christian Hospital Association in Malawi). It makes me even crosser (if there is such a word) that those who are most belligerent are those who sit all afternoon outside the lab. Doing nothing!"

But no one could doubt her love for her trainees, and evidence is adduced elsewhere of many ways in which she gave them practical as well as professional help. A contributing factor was her mastery of first Chichewa and then Chitumbuka; she knew these languages so well that she was able to really get to know the Malawian staff, patients and neighbours.

Sometimes Elizabeth had the unwelcome task of 'failing' students who hadn't done well enough. In one letter (to Joan and Martin Waldron; 19.11.87) she wrote,

"I had to keep four back this last time and that was a very traumatic time – two of them are still very sullen about it, and of course it is all *my* fault! Some of the girls always find it difficult as they think they know everything! I would like to see them all through for their own sakes – but then you have to think of the patients and that they are responsible for people's lives."

It was one of Elizabeth's dearest wishes to see the School of Nursing led by a Malawian Principal, employed by the Synod. In her Partner Plan letter of August 1991 she wrote,

> "With regard to the nursing school I would like to think that in the not too distant +-future I could hand over the responsibility of the school to a Malawian. I would ask for your prayers in this matter – that somewhere the Lord would be preparing someone for this task"

Her desire was, in that sense, to work herself out of a job. So, it was wonderful that she learned before her death of the appointment of Sister Desiree Mhango as Principal; her prayers had been granted. Elizabeth and Desiree had worked together and were good friends; the appointment brought Elizabeth great pleasure.

In her final official letter, printed and distributed by the Church's Board of World Mission, Elizabeth looked back on her service in Ekwendeni. The letter was published in December 1997, not long before her death. In it, she referred to the frustration of not being able to do as much as she wanted and to the fact that she missed the hustle and bustle of Ekwendeni. She looked back on 15 years filled with challenge, excitement and disappointments:

> "Seeing the new hospital come to reality, seeing the nursing school develop into a training school for nurses and midwives, seeing the development of Primary Health Care work and its many facets. Most important of all was seeing God's love continuing to grow among the people. There have been difficult times too, and your partnership and support in prayer and kind have enabled the work to continue through difficult as well as easy times. Thank you all".

The opening of the new hospital in 1986 was, naturally, a highlight of Elizabeth's time in Ekwendeni. In April 1986, she wrote,

> "By the first week in February all the bits and pieces that had to be done were finished off and we were given the keys."

She continued:

> "There were a hundred and one things to be done: theatre and Outpatients and laboratory and then the laundry. We had so much

sewing to do that we hired a tailor for two weeks and he sewed non-stop from 6 am till 6 pm Monday till Saturday, sewing curtains and sheets and covers and new mattress covers and pillow covers and lots of other things".

"The electricity still had to be checked, but it was decided that on 12th February we would start the move."

There was a frenzy of activity: cleaning and scrubbing and getting old mattresses covered and new ones out of the store and onto the beds.

"Then the equipment was moved from the male and female wards by the cart load or lorry load, depending which vehicle was at hand. Finally at 4 pm, the first of the patients. It was very exciting to be here".

The midwifery ward was opened the next day, and the first baby was born about two hours after the labour ward had moved. Elizabeth wrote,

"The whole place is looking very nice indeed and now that we have been in for some weeks, the surroundings too are beginning to look like hospital grounds rather than a building site, with new trees planted and flowers already in bloom."

Another very special occasion was the Centenary of the Mission in 1989. Elizabeth's description of the service of thanksgiving gives some insight into Malawian church life. The service was scheduled to begin at 10 am, but by 8.30 am the church was packed. The service that followed lasted 4 hours and 40 minutes!

"Many choirs sang and a family group from the nearby village sang and danced a very typical Ngoni song depicting the laying down of arms at the communion table in submission to Christ. This was very significant as the Ngoni were a warring nation at the time of the founding of the mission. Dada Hara, one of the old ministers, spoke of the history of the mission. Hymns were sung in Ngoni (Zulu), which few people speak now, Tumbuka, the present language, and English. The readings were in all three languages. Then followed two full-length sermons in Tumbuka and English. Throughout there was a real feeling of worship and rejoicing. I had the privilege of taking part in the service, which meant an uninterrupted view of all that was taking place. The service ended in an atmosphere of worship and rejoicing. As we look forward we seek prayer for the growth of the church in the next one hundred years, that it may continue to grow towards Christ".

At a later time Elizabeth would represent missionaries at another special service. It was held on 4th June 1996, marking 100 years since the death of William Koyi, a Zulu Christian who was instrumental in the first conversions among the Ngoni people. Elizabeth's Partner Plan letter of September 1996 described this occasion:

"We set off early in the morning and drove for what seemed a long time on dreadful roads to reach Njuyu. There many people had been gathering since early morning in an area near the graveyard – the many choirs, the Umanyano (Woman's Guild), ministers of the Livingstonia Synod, Chiefs and Sub-Chiefs, government officials and many villagers. The ceremony started with two dancers dressed as Ngoni warriors enacting the surrender of the Ngoni people to the gospel after a long time of warring and raiding. Then followed a service of praise and thanksgiving, a history of the bringing of the gospel to the Ngoni people, a speech by the present Chief, Chief Mbelwa, a grandson of the Mbelwa who brought this people to the gospel, choirs and dancing. A snake seen to be crawling up one of the trees disrupted the ceremony momentarily, but it was soon disposed of. After re-dedication and prayer we all walked quietly to the graveyard where people representing many organizations laid 26 wreaths. I had the privilege of representing the missionaries. Tribute was also paid to a George Rollo who is buried next to William Koyi. He came from Scotland and died after only three weeks in the mission field. We returned home in the dusk with Walter Chibambo (elder and preceptor in Ekwendeni) telling us many fascinating stories of the Ngoni and how the gospel has flourished in this area since".

Returning to Elizabeth's own particular sphere of work, there is no doubt that she was excited about the developments mentioned in the 1997 letter quoted earlier. This was the fact that

"All the heads of departments in the hospital and nursing school are Malawians. This is something we have prayed about for years. Please pray that they will continue in their posts."

That principle had been part of Christian mission in Malawi from the beginning. Hamish McIntosh (p.114) tells of Dr Laws speaking at the Free Church General Assembly in 1892, 17 years after the Livingstonia Mission had been established. The name was used at first for the whole work in the then Nyasaland and not only the station now known as Livingstonia. By the end of these 17 years Livingstonia had 32 schools with 7000 pupils. Laws appealed for more workers and more financial support and spoke of his own vision of African teachers and pastors being trained to teach others. He said,

"If Africa is to be won for Christ – and there is no 'if' about it for it will be – then the way to do it is by the Africans themselves."

Dr Laws attended a Conference on African Education in 1927. It met in Zomba and was called by the Governor, Sir Charles Bowring. According to Hamish McIntosh's account: "The Governor spoke of the occasion as a landmark on the eve of the Government's assuming control of educational policy." He paid tribute to the amount of educational work done by the missions compared with which the government's contribution up to date had been insignificant. The newly appointed Director of Education said at the conference that the aim of education should be 'the production of good, contented and loyal African citizens'. Dr Laws, when he spoke, expressed the aim of educational work rather differently: "Education", he said,

> "was intended to fit the individual to make the most of his life for the service of God, for his own good and for the good of his fellow men."

Elizabeth Mantell followed in Laws' footsteps. Her goal for her girls was that they should be enabled to make the most of their lives for the service of the Lord, for their own good and for the good of other people.

She was not greatly enamoured of administrative work; a letter to Ruth, written in March 1996, said: "This is Tuesday afternoon and we are about to sit down to a Management meeting – which I find thoroughly boring". However, Elizabeth recognised its importance; she was an active member of the CHAM Training Committee and she served on various other committees of the Nurses Council of Malawi and the Ministry of Health. It was through her efforts that Ekwendeni Training School was upgraded in 1991 from being a school of midwifery to a full training school.

But her particular ministry was with people. Dr Dorward writes of how:

> "The students had a champion for their cause in Liz in any discussion involving the School. She supported their personal development in a quiet way and had a genuine interest in their welfare and career. She wanted the best for them and expected them to give of their best in return. Their Christian growth was a deep concern. In the school Liz encouraged practical Christian living and ethics – with a careful cultural sensitivity."

She helped many people, including the ward maid who spoke of how Elizabeth had helped her obtain employment after she had been widowed.

On another occasion she commented that working with her students was no mere 7 am – 5 pm job:

> "In the middle of the night a few weeks ago I was wakened by some of the other students and asked to come and see Veronica who was crying and shouting and banging her head. She had just come back from

holiday and had been told that her best friend at school had died and it seemed as if she was 'possessed'. She was distraught. We prayed with her and sang with her through the night and eventually her heart was at peace. I was touched by the loving care of the other students. Veronica is a Christian – please pray that she will stay close to the Lord and not become disturbed again."

One imagines that, just as she was "touched by the loving care" of others, so the loving care of the Scots missionary would touch them.

Another incident reveals that Elizabeth's care extended far beyond what, officially, might have been expected. The letter, begun while the bath was running, related:

"11.45 pm. Well, it has been some evening. I ran the bath and then Ivy came in and chatted and had some cocoa. Then a posse of girls came up and said that M had left the hostel with her boyfriend and she was down at the trading centre! So I had to go down and find her. We went to the house – where people were all at a bar and dancing around the place – but no Mary. She was found at the bus station with her boyfriend and was trying to run away. I managed to persuade them to come to the hostel to discuss things! The boy had been drinking. He obviously wanted Mary for the night and off he would go with the bus tomorrow to Blantyre, leaving her high and dry."

She sought help from other members of the hospital staff, one of whom, as she baldly stated, 'threw him out!' Reflecting on it afterwards (did she ever get that bath?), she wrote:

"It is only by committing these things to the Lord that I can cope with them. Oh how good it is to realize the reality of the verses that tell us that the Lord says, 'Cast your care upon Me for I will sustain you'."

One of Elizabeth's extra-curricular activities was the Nurses' Christian Fellowship, which met on Sunday evenings. She was glad to be involved in this fellowship and sought to encourage her girls to grow in faith and discipleship even as they developed their professional nursing skills. She may not have spoken much of 'holistic' care, but holistic care was what she practiced; this was demonstrated by her concern for people not merely as bodies to be nursed but as people to be nurtured. It was this holistic approach that characterized her interaction with the girl students. Her involvement in the NCF was a major aspect of her pastoral and evangelistic work. She felt that students in Malawi were under the same pressures as students at home; and, she said, they needed our prayers. She found that the seed of God's word fell onto different kinds of soil; expressing herself in terms of the letter to the church of Laodicea (Revelation 3, 14-22), she wrote:

> "There are some very keen young Christians amongst them and some lukewarm and some decidedly cold!"

Involvement in Ekwendeni Church was, of course, a natural part of her life, and she gave services as an elder of the church. She was immensely respected by the church people who spoke of her affectionately, in the African manner, as 'our mother'.

Elizabeth was also respected in the mission station's school. Writing in March 1996, she told of having attended the opening of the newly renovated primary school. Different blocks had been named after different people who had had something to do with the rebuilding. Her self-deprecating manner is perhaps unconsciously revealed in her narrative:

> "The Headmaster asked if they could call one of the blocks after me – big joke!! – because quite a bit of money had come through me – but I'm afraid I said, 'No, thank you'! No way!"

She did accept the privilege of opening the new school by cutting the ribbon and unlocking the door.

And her hospitality! Hospitality was one of the many graces evidenced in Elizabeth's life. As stated elsewhere, it sometimes seemed that her khonde was never empty. However exhausted herself, she was always ready to make time for the many visitors who came seeking help, whether that help involved giving well considered financial assistance or providing a listening ear. She had a pastoral heart and many people found themselves drawn to her.

A paragraph from a letter written by Sister Carol Finlay who joined Elizabeth in Ekwendeni well illustrates this warm hospitality. Carol wrote:

> "Before I came to Malawi I heard so much from people in Scotland about Elizabeth Mantell, the Principal of the Nursing School at Ekwendeni. I knew that I was coming to work as the only other tutor at that time and I was a bit apprehensive. However when I arrived very late one night in April 1999, one of the first people to greet me was Sister Mantell. She said, 'Welcome to Ekwendeni; we are so happy to see you. Come in, have a cup of coffee, then there is hot water for a bath and your bed is ready'. I knew from that moment that we would be good friends, Liz and I."

Malawi's self-advertisement as "The Warm Heart of Africa" and the reputation of its people for friendliness, however, did not mean that there were never any pressures. For security purposes Elizabeth found it expedient to employ a watchman; she also owned a dog, named Jura. Jura has been described as a fine example of an Alsatian; Helen Donald remarks that a church service without the presence of Elizabeth and Jura was incomplete! Jura had been given to Elizabeth by an American couple whose dog had a litter. She was a large Alsatian with upright, pointed ears, a long nose and a sleek coat. She was said to be a very fussy dog and would eat only the best and most expensive dog food.

A guard dog was a good idea, because dangers did exist. This was highlighted in a particular incident in 1993. The Aberdeen *Evening Express* of 18th December that year referred to the incident, reported elsewhere in this book, with the headline, "Kirks pray for friend". Alongside a photograph of Elizabeth, the text read:

> "North-east churches are praying for the safety of a brave midwife caught up in dangerous unrest in Malawi. Troops hunting young rebels had entered the local church at Ekwendeni, and the following day Elizabeth escaped unharmed when she was threatened by a burglar who had broken into her home. Next night Irish nurse Elma Harkness was abducted but returned unhurt four hours later. Coupled with reports of shooting across the country the incidents have fuelled fears for Liz's safety."

Thankfully Elizabeth seemed to be none the worse for the incident.

Her diary allows us some insight into the trauma of that time. The entry for Monday 6th December 1993 records:

> "Carol set off to go to the Nurses' Christian Fellowship but was accosted at the bottom of her steps by a drunk man. She got such a fright. Came in for supper – then listened to a tape (service). Aileen and co. came up in a dreadful state a little while later to say Elma had screamed when she got into her house and then was taken away – disappeared. No reply in house. Carol and I went up for Rev Gondwe (Head of Station), then sent for police. Then got everyone out to search. Messages (were sent) to the British High Commission and Chris Wigglesworth (General Secretary of Board of World Mission), and phoned people at home to pray for her. We all prayed. Divided up into groups and searched the woods below Lay Training Centre. Then about 1 am she came running out of the dark, having got away from the man. He had taken her at knifepoint and gone away into the woods. But the Lord did indeed answer prayer. He bound the man and he did no harm. She showed remarkable presence of mind. In the house afterward all the police and Synod people came and then we had a time of prayer and

thanksgiving. Once everyone left, we had a coffee and then bed about 3 am. So thankful that the ending was such. Elma stayed with me"

The next day's entry says, "Elma slept a little and she really is wonderful".

Other difficulties she encountered were sometimes mentioned in her letters. After we had visited in August 1996, she wrote on 10th November very shortly before being taken ill, "Since you left at the end of August, the house has never stopped!" Another letter referred to a visit from a former colleague, adding that the latter had brought seven other people with her: "So the house resembled a students' hostel for a few days". Her penchant for hospitality sometimes exhausted her, though she didn't show it to her visitors.

The heat was another difficulty. In that same letter Elizabeth wrote about 'candles beginning to lean over, the dog lying around all day and the flowers drying up.'

That dog was Mac, first mentioned in June 1996. Jura, who had been Elizabeth's faithful guard-dog and companion, had died and it took a considerable amount of thought before she decided to obtain another dog.

> "Friends had a puppy which they offered me. I did wonder if I would have the time and patience to deal with it. Well, for the first few weeks I wondered what I had done as she was a very timid creature, running away whenever anyone approached her, jumping up whenever she saw me returning from work and all the other things that go along with trying to housetrain a dog!! However she has become a very calm little dog now and no longer does a detour when anyone approaches us as we walk down the road."

We vividly remember times when Elizabeth would put Mac out of the swing door at the front of her khonde, only for the said creature to run round to the side of the house, jump over the fence and reappear.

Our account has emphasised the busyness of Elizabeth's life; she drove herself and seldom had much time to herself. However, it was not all work and no play, and several correspondents mention times of great fun and laughter. Stella Eusebio, for example, speaks of still having a tape made one Hogmanay in Mulanje, with Liz and others reciting "Auld Maid in a Garret"!

A helpless female she certainly was not! Over the years she turned her hand to many matters, which would have been outside the remit of a sister tutor in Great Britain. She was adept at dealing with the insects that might have scared a more timid person. Iain Craighead tells of a rat falling through the ceiling one day as she was serving lunch, 'but she was quite unfazed';

Lindsey Malcolm similarly tells of an enormous, multi-coloured, bird-eating spider that appeared above her cistern, which Elizabeth (and Arthur Buck) 'bravely killed with a flip-flop each.

One thing that did faze Elizabeth was a snake! She would tell of an occasion when camping at Vwaza Marsh when she found a snake inside her tent and was terrified until it was dealt with. On another occasion we remember sitting as passengers in her car, manoeuvring the switchback Gorodi Road south from Livingstonia, when we spotted a mamba by the roadside. One of our company was about to open the door in order to take a photograph when Elizabeth more or less screamed at her to shut it immediately; she had heard stories of snakes insinuating themselves around car exhausts or lurking in wheel arches, waiting for an opportunity to strike.

Returning to people, however, Shena Dougall, who went to work in Ekwendeni Hospital in 1989 found that, although Elizabeth was her junior by 20 years, she took Shena under her wing. Shena lived 'through the wall' in the other half of the house and:

"...although we always respected each other's privacy, I knew I could depend on her to advise me on any problems, and when either of us needed a confidante we shared our troubles".

Shena's account refers to many happy evenings playing her favorite game, "Scramble"; my researches have not elucidated much about this variation of Scrabble, but Shena recounts,

"The local joke was that Elizabeth had friends in to enjoy good conversation. People passing her window could hear the constant sound of voices saying, 'Take one, take one."

This referred not to food or drink but to the Scrabble tiles.

Titchui Chan worked at Ekwendeni for four years and remarks that she stopped on her way home every day so that she could talk things over with Elizabeth who would pray with and for her.

Titchui also fondly recalls laughing with Elizabeth when she arrived home to find ensconced an elderly and homeless Malawian lady who often enjoyed Elizabeth's hospitality. On this occasion she had put all her clothes to soak in Elizabeth's bath-tub while she liberally sampled the toiletries – totally naked but unabashed!

Helen Donald speaks for many in saying:

"To work with Elizabeth and count ourselves among her wide circle of friends was a privilege. Frequently we recall humorous occasions in her company, for we shared many jokes and with her help could laugh at ourselves. She still holds a special place in our memories."

Chapter 7

The Correspondent

Elizabeth was a letter writer *extraordinaire*. A fairly typical conclusion to one of her Partner Plan letters said:

"There are many of you to whom I owe letters. Please be patient; you will get a reply sometime in the not too distant future."

All attempts to persuade her that people were happy to write without necessarily expecting a reply were in vain; she had a great desire to keep up with her correspondence.

This chapter will consist largely of excerpts from her letters, which reveal many aspects of her life in Malawi. Elizabeth led a very busy life in the hospital and the mission station; she was not one to sit idle. But life was not "all work and no play". Her letters reveal a delight in the beauties of God's creation and an enjoyment of many trips and escapades.

One of her personal letters started:

"I am writing this in an evening when the moon is shining so brightly that it is almost like daylight. Last night we had a similar night but up in Nyika Plateau – when we kept hoping that maybe in the moonlight we would see leopard, but No! – Not even its cough was heard. Stewart (my nephew) and his friend are on holiday at the moment. We all rattled our way up to Nyika Plateau for the weekend. It is such a lovely place to visit, but very cold at this time of year. We saw very little game, but the journey up and back proved to be full of adventure, with a puncture, a broken exhaust, the wing mirror falling off and finally the battery packing up – but the Lord saw us there and back safely."

In 1993, Elizabeth wrote:

"October and the hot season has begun. Dust flies everywhere. Leaves are found in all the corners. Everywhere is covered with layers of dust an hour after cleaning. Feet are dusty and dirty as soon as we step out on to the road. We realize what a feeling of well-being there must have been when in Jesus' time visitors' feet were washed as a gesture of welcome. It is a pity that this is still not the custom today."

That same letter went on to describe two situations, which show that a missionary's lot is not always a happy one. She described it as a spiritual battle:

> "This week we have been very aware of the many tactics that can be used against the work of the Lord. One of them being despondency – and we could have known plenty of that this week. One of our colleagues, Alice Duthie, has had to be flown home due to illness; a break-in to Ann Dawson's house while she was out at the prayer meeting; and last but not least the threat of the hospital staff going on strike.
>
> "Yet throughout all this time we have felt the hand of the Lord guiding and strengthening as lovingly He has steered us through one of the most difficult weeks we have had here in Ekwendeni."

After this, there followed the words of Annie J. Flint's hymn:

> He giveth more grace, as the burdens grow greater,
>
> He sendeth more strength when the labours increase;
>
> To added affliction He addeth more mercy,
>
> To multiplied trials His multiplied peace.

She went on to describe a situation that caused her much heartache:

> "We have gone through a time here that I thought we would never go through – a time when many of the hospital staff have threatened to go on strike. A strike in a mission hospital seemed unthinkable!"

She wrote of the genuine grievances that staff had, as the government had raised the salaries of its own medical staff without giving consideration to people working in CHAM (Christian Health Association of Malawi) hospitals:

> "Many of the staff members, led by a few stronger ones, said that unless the government came up with the money for the new scales and the arrears, then as from 11th October they would not work until their requests were met. After many meetings, letters, phone calls and faxes, the government promised to pay. This unfortunately did not satisfy the staff, as they wanted to see evidence of the money. Many of us felt this was now an unreasonable demand, as we all know that things do not happen overnight in Africa!! No matter – the money had to be there by a certain date and if not then the strike would be on and it looked as if the patients did not matter. Those who felt this was wrong argued with

the hard-liners, but to no avail. Finally the Medical coordinator went to the Ministry and he obtained the money. Meanwhile the General Secretary of the Synod talked for a whole afternoon to the staff. At the eleventh hour the strike was averted."

Elizabeth's high standards of professionalism, linked with compassion, led her to feel a great sense of disappointment at these events. She wrote:

"We are supposed to be ambassadors for Christ, so what kind of witness was this? This is a newfound freedom, as never before have the people been allowed to express their feelings in this way. What has to be learned, though, is that with freedom also comes responsibility."

Not all letters were taken up with such serious matters. In November 1993, she described an enjoyable holiday:

"After Carol came back from leave, Margaret and I went on holiday to Zimbabwe and had a wonderful week. We flew to Harare, had two nights in a luxury hotel before flying off to the Victoria Falls. We stayed at the Victoria Falls Hotel. This hotel was built back in colonial days and has an air of quiet efficiency and old-fashioned comfort with superb food, and yet is modern and up to date. Everything worked and our every need was catered for. Unashamedly I enjoyed every minute of it. The view from the terrace was over green lawns surrounded by magnificent bougainvillea bushes in rich reds and purples and oranges, down into the Zambezi gorge and over to the Victoria Falls railway bridge which spans the gorge joining the two countries of Zimbabwe and Zambia. We had a flight over the Falls, and oh! how I wish David Livingstone could have seen them in this way. One day we walked across the bridge to see the Falls from the Zambian side. While walking across the bridge we watched some folks "no' right in the heid" doing the ever popular bungee jumping. What people do for kicks!! With that bit of excitement behind us we went on to Hwange, the game park, where we stayed at Sikumi Tree Lodge. This was a small camp run by a private group. The wooden chalets were built in the trees and were comfortable with all mod-cons, even to an electric blanket in the bed – and it was cold enough for us to need it! We ate under the stars and beside campfires. Game viewing was wonderful. We even saw cheetah."

Another trip took place on 9th October 1994 when Elizabeth and Ruth visited the church at Eutini, about fifty miles east of Ekwendeni. In her home town of Macduff there had been a union of the previously separate congregations (Doune and Gardner) and this resulted in there being some surplus communion silver. It was decided to give this to a Malawian congregation, and when Elizabeth visited Eutini:

"We were welcomed warmly by the Umanyano (Woman's Guild) and Men's Guild singing and dancing. There then followed a simple but meaningful service. It was nice that Ruth, my sister, was able to be there too and it was very moving as the elements were brought in to think back on the times they had been carried in these very same vessels in the church in Macduff where she had been brought up. We were very aware that 'We are all one in Christ Jesus'."

Ruth wrote about it also in her diary:

"This was the first time they had used the Gardner communion cups. The service was in Tumbuka but I could make out that we were to read Haggai 1 and 2 Corinthians 8, 1-15. This, Mr Mhone told me later, was what he based the sermon on to encourage people to be liberal to the church. Mind you, in an area like this there are many people who have so little to be liberal with. It was so hot that Mr Mhone was dripping with perspiration dressed as he was in dog-collar, full suit and vest and robes" (hadn't he read Ezekiel 44,18b then!). "I love when the elements are carried in by the elders, singing as they come in, and then the congregation joins them in singing, *"Mwana mberere, wati yeghera, Zakwananga zite zose"* (The Lamb of God takes away all our sins). Although the church was full (400 – 500) and most sitting in lines on the floor, communion was served reverently but efficiently. I was so glad to see the Gardner cups being used and appreciated. Of course, there were speeches of thanks, and Elizabeth and I both had to reply and bring greetings from Scotland. We were asked to bring greetings back to our church and were also told not to forget them. After the service a collection was taken for a bed for the manse! We were given a delicious meal of chicken meat, rice, nsima, mango and tea prepared by some ladies."

Some of Elizabeth's letters would give graphic descriptions of the sights and sounds of Malawi. It might be, as in one letter:

"The rain drumming on the roof - and it is music to the ears. Along with the rain the frogs start up and all kinds of other night sounds that are special to Africa."

Or it might be in the hot season:

"When sitting on the khonde I look out to the distant hills. The golden shower, a beautiful bright orange in colour cascades over the eaves and the pink begonia is just in front of it. The purple jacaranda is in full bloom and the dropped flowers make a carpet of the most beautiful hue on the ground. The brown road winds into the distance, disappearing into the blue hills which are nearly obliterated by the haze."

Other letters would reveal some of the stresses and strains that affected her life and work. Life was not easy; apart from the constant busyness, there was the pressure of seeking to maintain good relationships, both among Malawian staff and students and also with other expatriate staff.

There could also be health issues. Although Elizabeth seemed to keep in good health, there were times when she fell victim to illness, as revealed in a letter written in September 1984. She wrote about having a good weekend:

> "Despite having had fever off and on during the weekend. I think I had a bite which had got infected and I had fever off and on for about a week – Temp. going up to 103 at times. But I managed to cope without having to go to bed by dosing myself with aspirin. I feel very tired this week and I think it may be the after-effects of that. At any rate, there is no rest"

And she goes on to tell of a colleague being on holiday for the following two weeks:

> "So that means two nights a week 'on call' – and the ward is getting very busy!"

In November 1993 Elizabeth wrote amusingly about some of her students who had not arrived back on schedule.

> "The excuses for not coming back on time were as varied as they were imaginative: grandfather has died (even though they had been to his funeral sometime last year); the bus broke down and they had to sleep at Mzimba (which often happens); they were sick with malaria (it takes three days to get over this in Ekwendeni but two weeks to get over it at home); they were waiting for transport money (forgetting that they had been given a concession ticket). I think that some of the girls forget that we were not born yesterday!"

When back in Scotland, she continued to enjoy the sights of God's creation. In the summer of 1997 she wrote:

> "Macduff couldn't look better. As the sun shines on the blue sea we watch the dolphins swimming in the bay and the white-sailed yachts out to see them more closely. Then in the evening as we walk round to the lighthouse the sun sets, making a golden pathway over the sea and a fishing boat heads out for a night's work. It is beautiful and we are reminded of God's glory. I have so much enjoyed these summer days."

Sadly these were to be her last summer days in this world. In November 1996 she had taken ill and had been flown back to the UK for treatment. In the same letter she referred to chemotherapy treatment she was receiving, before telling of journeys to attend the Nurses' Christian Fellowship Conference in Crieff, Lesley Thompson's commissioning service and then a holiday with Ruth at their beloved Achiltibuie on the west coast of Scotland.

"Unfortunately since then I have not been as well as hoped and last week was in hospital for further investigation. Now I await the result and hope it will not mean my going into hospital again. As we go into the future please continue to pray that I will be given the strength to cope with whatever it holds. One thing I do know – and that is that we are in God's hands."

She also wrote of being overwhelmed and greatly strengthened by the letters, cards and visits of so many friends and wrote, amazingly: "This has been a good time", adding, "I would wish that everyone who has been in my position could have the loving support that I have experienced".

Chapter 8

The Diarist

Although Elizabeth often spoke and wrote about feeling tired, she liked to keep her diary up to date. I am very grateful to the family for allowing me access to these diaries. She used "The College Diary", which has a page for every day, and would sometimes fill the complete page with a hand-written account of what had been happening. Sometimes she would miss several days or even weeks and then take it up again.

As one who keeps a diary only to record engagements, I have found it fascinating to read the words in which Elizabeth would sometimes confide in her diary, writing on essentially private matters. On occasions, it reads almost like a prayer-diary as she addresses not the abstract page but the living One she called her Lord.

This chapter will consist of extracts from these diaries. They range from the profound:

> "We are not put into the world to solve every problem, but we are here to make Christ's presence felt. I pray that we are able to do that". (17.4.87)

to the sometimes very forthright, such as this comment, made after a furlough visit to the Gallery of Modern Art in Edinburgh:

> "had lunch there (some dreadful pictures!)" (13.11.86),

and from the deeply-felt:

> "Will need to spend more time with the Lord" (24.1.91)

to the matter-of-fact:

> "Fell asleep after getting rid of a mouse in my bed" (26.10.90)

Many of these excerpts will confirm assertions made elsewhere in the book about Elizabeth. For instance, it has been said that Africa was in her blood, and it is revealing to find the entry for Friday 9th January 1987, the day after she returned to Ekwendeni: "Wakened at 8 am. Sun shining – very hot. Lovely sounds and smells of Africa".

The diaries also reveal that she did not keep social hours. Thursday 26th February 1987: "Wakened 3 am – did some more marking – coffee. 4 am – read the good Book. Fell asleep till 7 am. Late for prayers".

A few weeks later, on Wednesday 8th April of that year, she wrote:

> "Called at 1.30 am to prem. baby – NND – and also to see a prem who would not allow the staff nurse to examine her. But was in 2nd stage so I delivered her and she really was quite good in the end – just a very frightened person. Was up till 4 am. Had about 1½ hours sleep and then on duty".

Fatigue is mentioned often in her diary:

- "Did not feel like teaching - but committed it to the Lord and had a really good day" (24.3.87).
- 5.12.87: "Very tired and down all day. Felt I am not handling nurses well. Had a good cry".
- 9.12.87: "Prayer meeting – but everyone too tired to participate".
- 11.2.88: "I am just so tired". This was followed by three days running where the only entry was, "Too tired and busy".
- 6.1.90: "Irritable all day. Should not have been late last night" (the previous day's entry revealed that she had taken down her Christmas decorations in the evening and watched the video, 'Casablanca,' till very late).

Such entries reveal something of the fatigue that beset Elizabeth; on one occasion she even wrote: "Wakened up tired". But the nature of the work was, of course, very demanding. Excerpts such as those given above show that she often had to make do with few hours of sleep. On Monday 25th January 1988, she recorded:

> "Busy all night. One patient with breech presentation – large baby? Called doctor at 2 am – said cx was 8 cm dilated. But I did it 2 hrs later – only 6 cm. So we sectioned her at 6 am. So it was a long night. Back for breakfast at 6.30 am and went to bed for 2 hours. Then on duty."

No wonder she would sometimes write things like:

> "Had a long frustrating day. Don't think I can take much more of this!!" (3.7.91)

Her inanimate diary would often feel the brunt of that tiredness and even frustration, as on an occasion when she started to write a letter and then had problems.

> "Decided to get a circular letter done – so went to do it on word processor. Took all morning to do it - did a few copies and then lunchtime, and then more in afternoon. Wiped the whole thing off and it took me all afternoon to put it in again. Then copied till 6 pm (was very frustrated)."

Her hospitality is reflected in the simple entry for a day in 1992 (24th October): "Lunch table – full; Tea table – full".

In addition to all such pressures, Elizabeth felt the pressure of dealing with her nurses, sometimes lending a listening ear and helping with their problems, but also sometimes having, in honesty, to fail some of them so far as their training was concerned. So on 7.5.87 she would tell the diary:

> "Had the seniors today. Did Outpatients and took all morning to do it! Then spent the afternoon giving them back their papers. Had to tell 3 of them they would have to re-sit next week. Just hate doing this, but do not think they will _ever_ make it. Then had to speak to X re her work on A/N which had not been good. I hate always having to tell them off."

On another occasion, she recorded that she:

> "Had to speak to M and W as neither are pulling their weight."

On Friday 8th January 1988 she wrote:

> "Teaching Finalists in pm, but they are really hard going and am exhausted with them. Wonder how long I can carry on this way – being so tired."

Thankfully there were other times when she could record, as on 8.11.93:

> "Results came out today. All our girls passed".

On Tuesday 11th September 1990, she confided in her diary that she was just into the bath when she was called to do an assessment delivery. It was:

> "much better than last time but still not brilliant".

Other issues would sometimes arise. The diary entry for 18.10.87 tells of one nurse coming to complain about her off-duty hours:

> "Lost my temper with her - felt really bad, but it seemed like last straw!!! Church - did not wait for communion. Really need to see M first."

Nor was it only the nurses who caused her grief. On 9.2.88 she wrote:

> "The meeting (of Senior Staff) went on for ages. They seem to talk about nothing!" and the entry for 23.1.96 simply says, "Boring Medical Board all day!"

Sometimes issues with colleagues were recorded in the diary. An entry for September 1993, for example, told of a disagreement with a fellow-missionary. Elizabeth's self-reflection ran:

> "She has found me difficult these last 5 months, and I have found the same too. Disappointing. But we have to make a go. We both have to look at ourselves."

Of whom was she thinking, I wonder, when she wrote, after coming back from a Bible Study meeting:

> "Jonah was a 'grumpy' person, but was chosen by God and did God's will."

There were occasions when she would commiserate with others, as when a colleague came to her in her office, very upset:

> "Went to her house after. Talked and cried but we prayed about it in the end. How good it is to commit things to the Lord."

Early in this book it was stated that part of Elizabeth's specialness lay in her refusal to believe that she was anything out of the ordinary. Indeed, her diaries show a constant awareness that she had much room for progress in Christ-like living. On Sunday 6th April 1987 she woke up at 6 am and had coffee and toast in bed while she listened to a service from her home congregation in Macduff. The message was from Proverbs:

> "God's Word – we should be steeped in it! I pray that I will – and that I will not be selfish and jealous of things and people."

On 17th December of that year she confided to her diary:

> "Have not spent much time in the Lord's presence the last two days – and feel in need of it. I pray that I would have a real thirst for His word."

Later, in January 1990, she wrote:

> "Reading – Nehemiah 9, 22-37. 'We cannot undo the past or guarantee the future but we are responsible for today. Let's give ourselves to God this day in penitence and unreserved commitment. Love so amazing, so divine demands… my all'. I pray that I will abide by this."

And in September the following year she rhetorically asked her diary,

"What have I done for the Lord today?"

On 14th September 1993 she wrote about going to Bible Study but somehow finding it difficult to feel part of the fellowship:

"Came back and read quietly God's word alone".

Some of these entries confirm what has previously been said in these pages: missionaries do not always feel spiritually on top of the world. Elizabeth's inner struggle reveals the heart of someone who was not content simply to do her job well; she had a passion to become a more Christ-like person. My wife and I recall an incident when we visited Vwaza Marsh and there was some conversation between Elizabeth and the girl at the gate. We couldn't understand what was being said, of course, and it was only in reading her diaries that I found her own account of what took place:

"...Entrance fee now K75 non-resident and K15 for residents. Girl at the gate would not believe I was a resident and got cross with her! What kind of witness am I?"

The diaries also tell of her share in the life of the church in Ekwendeni. On Sunday 13th August 1989 she recorded:

"Had a long lie and finished letter to Ruth. Then went with Sheena to Tumbuka service – quite enjoyed it – even understood some of it!"

On another occasion she wrote with frank honesty:

"Went to Church. Mr X preaching – not a good word to say about missionaries!"

And in 1991, when she had been inducted as an elder of the congregation:

"Went to Tumbuka service. I understood nearly all of the service and sermon – then had to go up to be introduced to the congregation as a new elder".

Elizabeth's diary entries were by no means all downbeat or despondent. She had an eye for a bit of fun too. Here is a pasted-in cutting headed "Breakfast Prayer":

"English version: Lord, grant that we may not be like porridge – stiff, stodgy and hard to stir, but like Cornflakes – crisp, fresh and ready to serve. Scottish version: Lord, grant that we may not be like Cornflakes – lightweight, brittle and cold, but like porridge – warm, comforting and full of goodness".

Inserted between the pages for December 1989 is a typed sheet headed "Ekwendeni Christmas Song". Unfortunately, it does not give the tune, but the chorus ran:

> Ekwendeni Hospital cares for everybody;
>
> The doctors groan and the sisters moan and the nurses will not study.
>
> (...)
>
> Dr Dorward treats his patients with a perfect bedside manner,
>
> But we all know his favorite toy is his new sonic scanner.
>
> Miss Mantell has the students all in terror for their poor lives,
>
> But when she's finished teaching them they'll all be perfect midwives.

Elizabeth would also tell her diary when she wasn't feeling too well. On Monday 24th August 1987 she wrote:

> "Wakened at 6 am with colic and nausea and nearly fainted in the bathroom. It all settled by 7.30 am, but just wanted to sleep then and went to bed. Had to cancel classes. Slept off and on all day and did corrections".

Then came the time when Elizabeth took ill and had to be brought home. On Sunday 10th November 1996 she wrote:

> "Church – it was an awful sermon – on how much to give for the Presbytery office – which has to be completed. Coffee, then tried to write some letters. Not feeling well."

That "not feeling well" was the first indication her diary received that something was really wrong. The last thing she wrote in her diary, on Thursday 14th November that year, dealt with ordinary matters. It mentioned "Paper III Midwifery" and then simply said:

> "Went to Belinda to ask her to take prayers in am".

Let me conclude this chapter with a few further entries from Elizabeth's diaries, on assorted matters:

- Sunday 15th July 1990 (while on furlough): "Rev Grahame Walker (former minister of Doune Church, Macduff) preaching today. Lovely to see him back – 32 years since he first came to Macduff. He was instrumental in bringing me to the Lord".

- 6.12.90: "M came along from Guides. She had her uniform on. We had a good time – reef knot, clove hitch and made a ladder. How to tie a triangle bandage. Coloured in map".

- 24.12.90 (Nativity play): "All ready – but two of the nurses did not turn up – so had to pick new shepherds and innkeeper at last minute. Play went OK. Hope the message got through".

- 21.5.91: "Blantyre. After breakfast took the car to Mandala Motors and left it to be seen to. Walked across the road to Mandala House, built in 1891 – now used as offices. Looked into the cupboards – saw old photos and found one with Dad in it. Was thrilled".

- 16.9.91: "FIRST DAY OF NEW TRAINING. A little bit of history. 13 girls started. Had the Junior Midwives early - left 10 am. Then we had an introductory block:

    Welcome

    Committed it all to the Lord

    Introduction

    Filling in charts

    Meeting of senior staff members

    Uniforms, books, rule and regulations

    Show round hospital

- 4.2.92: "Still no electricity – it is apparently a nation-wide failure. Since there is no power the water pumps are not working so already the water situation is bad especially at the hospital and the hostel".

- 2.4.93: "Hostel – showed girls 'Charlie Chaplin' and 'Jesus of Nazareth (part 2)'."

Chapter 9
The Hostess

As it has been mentioned earlier, one of Elizabeth's great gifts was hospitality. Her house in Ekwendeni was a place of welcome; passers-by would often see assorted people gathered on the khonde at the front of the house. Tired as she often was herself and essentially a private person, Elizabeth was always prepared to make time for people.

One year, as she looked forward to Christmas, she mentioned in an undated card that Ruth, who had arrived in November, was:

Elizabeth coming from work with her house on the background

"The 38th visitor to have stayed in this house or the one next door since January! It is just as well Carol Finlay (who occupied the house next door) has been on leave!"

This spirit of hospitable friendship has been expressed in a little poem simply called, "Liz". It was found among Elizabeth's papers but I have been unable to discover who the author was:

We all have a friend called Liz Mantell
Who runs her house like the Ritz Hotel;
Coffees and lunches and afternoon teas –
'Come in; you're real welcome – just be at your ease'.

There's a library service, a wide range of books,
A hairdressing service for improving your looks,
And if ticks should bite you in some awkward parts,
Then Liz will remove them – it's one of her arts.

There's a chauffeuring service for going away,
Scrabble and things to amuse if you're coming to stay –
Like me – ken ye Doric? Well, I lached til I grat
At Liz's collection of 'Scotland the What'.

But if you have troubles and worries galore,
The future uncertain, your poor head so sore,

Then pour out your troubles to Liz who will be
Your very best friend in adversity.

For, whatever the problem, whatever the need,
Some help will be given – it will; yes, indeed;
And she's quite sure to pray with you and lead
To the One Whom she loves, Who supplies all our needs.

My wife and I were at the receiving end of this generous hospitality when Elizabeth opened her home to us for the month of August 1996. Before I knew anything about it, she had received a phone call from the Session Clerk of Macduff Church about the possibility of the church sending its minister and his wife to Malawi on a pastoral visit to her. The occasion was to be in celebration of the 25th anniversary of my ordination, the congregation would mark the occasion by sending me away! They would gift the flight tickets and so on, and Elizabeth would be our hostess. The visit was to be partly a holiday, but also a pastoral visit, during which I would have many opportunities to minister to both missionaries and Malawians.

Elizabeth was eager to welcome the possibility. In the course of our four weeks' stay, she arranged for me to preach on three Sundays; give three addresses at a retreat for missionaries; speak three times at the Hospital Christian Fellowship; conduct three staff Bible studies; take a school assembly and conduct hospital prayers on three occasions. I was introduced in one church as the first white minister ever to preach there. Nan, my wife, also shared in various meetings.

We also managed to see something of the country. Elizabeth drove us about over mostly very rough roads, and we enjoyed some time by Lake Malawi, at places such as Sambani Lodge. At Vwasa Marsh we viewed a remarkable variety of wildlife: hippos, kudu, impala, fish eagles, velvet monkeys, baboon, blacksmith plover and countless more.

We quickly discovered that Elizabeth was held in very high regard in Malawi. She was anxious, as were the other missionaries we met, not to be put on any pedestal, yet there is no doubt that she demonstrated a degree of self-sacrificing commitment that was an inspiration to behold. Ordinary she might be, but she was giving extraordinary service in Ekwendeni, first to Christ as the Lord she served, and then to the people around her.

Writing in our local newspaper after the visit, we found ourselves reflecting that, if anyone should be in any doubt about whether Christianity makes a difference or does any good in the world, they would do well to visit Ekwendeni. There they would see no theoretical kind of faith, no do-nothing religion that treats Christianity as an intellectual philosophy. The whole mission station there is a wonderful demonstration of practical Christianity, and Elizabeth herself was very much part of that.

Ezekiel 47 has a wonderful vision of a stream of life-giving water flowing from the new temple in Jerusalem. The river came from the place of sacrifice in the sanctuary and flowed down from there, bringing life and vitality wherever it went. Although there were no tributaries, the river kept growing deeper and fuller all the way; the presence of tributaries would have negated the vision's message about the blessing coming from one source only. Part of Ezekiel's vision was:

> "I saw a great number of trees on each side of the river. He (Ezekiel's angelic guide) said to me, 'This water flows towards the eastern region and goes down to the Arabah, where it enters the Sea. When it empties into the Sea, the water there becomes fresh. Swarms of living creatures

will live wherever the river flows. There will be large numbers of fish, because this water flows there and makes the salt water fresh; so where the river flows everything will live'."

Such was Ezekiel's vision of the blessing that would abound wherever God's river would flow, and so it has been. It may be true that there have been some terrible things done in the name of Christianity, yet it remains also true that the gospel of Christ has brought innumerable blessings to this world.

I recall W.E. Sangster's lovely story of a traveller coming upon a tribe of moon-worshippers. He was surprised and remarked that he had heard of sun-worshippers before but, moon-worshippers...? The tribes-people's reply was:

"Well, the sun shines in the daytime when there's plenty of light anyway, but the clever moon shines at night when it's dark and we're badly in need of some light."

We live in the wonderful light of God all the time.

In particular, healthcare and education have been trees that have grown on the banks of this river of life. This has been true in Malawi as elsewhere. The work of the hospital, in its many aspects, has been described already, including Elizabeth's emphasis on training others to multiply her own work. Of course, education is also very important. We visited the local primary school, where 2050 pupils are taught in shifts. The 73 teachers were doing their very best for the pupils, despite working in conditions that, by western standards, were very poor indeed. One teacher had a plank for his desk and no desks for the children. We had taken various articles with us, including some pencils, rulers and other items from Macduff Primary School; these were all received as if they had been made of gold. We also visited the girls' Secondary School, an establishment run with tremendous efficiency by Anne Dawson, then head-teacher. Elizabeth also showed us round the Lay Training Centre, the Blind School and the College of Commerce. All of these educational establishments were developed as part of the mission station and as an outcome of the gospel message of One, who said:

"Inasmuch as you did it for the least of my brethren, you did it for me"
(Matthew 25, 40).

Associated with the hospital is a factory where special maize/soya porridge is produced; there is also a grain bank. Mobile clinics visit outlying districts, caring especially for mothers and babies. At one of these clinics we observed a health education talk, with various teaching songs being sung with great enthusiasm. We also saw the queues of mothers waiting to have their babies weighed and inoculated - many as a result of a widely publicized drive to 'kick polio out of Malawi' - or to receive medication and much-valued food supplements.

We visited the Relief and Development Project, which majors on sustainable development: promoting the growth of nutritionally valuable crops and the rearing of poultry, rabbits and pigs. And it was a particular joy to visit a shallow wells project, where we saw Ezekiel's vision come to fruition in a literal way.

Douglas Willis, on one of his visits to Malawi, saw the completion of one such project. His expressive account is worth quoting at some length:

"On an early morning visit to a village to the north of Ekwendeni, the sun was hardly rising as we set off from the hospital in a Land Rover with Kistone at the wheel, sharing the inside of the vehicle with all the bits and pieces required for the latest shallow well project. The hospital has had a long and successful Programme of shallow wells where water can be obtained from underground sources that are not too deep. Where the water table is high, a well of no great depth allows water to percolate through the ground and gather at the bottom. With the aid of a simple metal hand pump, the village women can then raise water that is clean and safe."

An Ambulance which she donated to Ekwendeni Mission Hospital

He goes on to describe the arrival at the site of the new well and the subsequent build-up to the moment when the pump could be attached and clean water would flow:

> "Soon everything was ready and many more women gathered excitedly at the spot. The round concrete capping was manhandled into place, revealing the date and the inscription, 'Glory to God'. It took no time to install the pump and then a hush of expectation fell as one of the men started to work the handle up and down.

Elizabeth 2nd from left with her family members

In a few minutes there was a buzz of excitement and then a chorus of ululating from the women as clear water began to spring forth from the mouth of the pump. The dirty, unsafe water supply has been replaced by a reliable source that was clean and free from water-borne infection. There was great rejoicing as the project was completed and the women gathered with their buckets and clay pots to collect water from the village's new well. The day had begun with discolored, unsafe supplies being drawn from a stagnant pool and now, as the fast-dipping sun was intensifying the red of the surrounding countryside, it was ending with clear water gushing from the pump as freshly as if it was springing out of a rock face."

This had been one more demonstration of that practical Christianity which gives the lie to the notion that Christianity is all talk and no action. Here, in the most literal sense, was living water and work that had been done in the name of One who spoke of being able to give living water to those who are thirsty (John 4, 14).

Elizabeth was anxious that we should see as much as possible of this work. However, one of the things we discovered was that missionaries could sometimes feel, spiritually, quite dry. There seemed to be some missionaries who regarded themselves as being in Malawi to do a job, in healthcare or whatever, but without any very high commitment to explicitly Christian work, fellowship and mission.

We were surprised, for example, when we were visited one Sunday afternoon by a group of missionaries on their way back from a weekend away, and realised that they had made no effort to be in church that day. We found ourselves wondering what their sending churches would think if they knew of the omission. Perhaps this remark may seem hard on the missionaries, especially when one takes into account such problems with church attendance as language difficulties, sometimes rather staid singing and a mixed standard of preaching. Nevertheless, should not missionary staff be completely identified with their local church, established with so much effort by their forerunners and which, despite difficulties and weaknesses (failings shared with churches everywhere) is seeking to hold up the light of Christ? Elizabeth herself and some of the others set a good example of such identification and involvement with the church, and was highly respected within the fellowship of the church in Ekwendeni.

People at home in the UK might imagine that missionaries inhabit a permanent spiritual high, but we discovered something which should have come as no surprise: that they are subject to the same kinds of ups and downs as Christian people everywhere. Indeed, missionaries have to contend with the added issue of sometimes feeling a lack of fellowship and also of teaching. Obviously, language can be an issue; during her Mlanje days, Elizabeth had been more fluent in Chichewa, spoken in the south of the country, than she became in the Tumbuka language of Ekwendeni. And, language aside, it is sometimes felt that there is not the strength of systematic teaching ministry in the field that missionaries may have enjoyed at home.

We discovered this during informal fellowship times in Elizabeth's house, when she would enjoy a session with our Bibles open. On these occasions she would ask that we simply minister to her, and also in Bible Studies with other expatriate staff. Missionaries, like other Christians, can be subject to spiritual problems, doubts and dryness; like all Christians, they are "earthen vessels" (2 Corinthians 4, 7). The Bible has always warned that we are engaged in a spiritual battle in which our enemies are not merely flesh and blood but "the spiritual forces of evil in the heavenly realms" (Ephesians 6:12). No doubt it serves the devil's purposes if he can bring front-line workers into a position of defeat; however, we would not credit the devil with God-like power, for 1 John 4, 4 remains true: "Greater is he that is in you than he that is in the world".

Thanks to the work of the early pioneers, Malawi has long been what might be called a Christianised society. However we also discovered that faith in Christ sometimes seems to coexist with belief in witchcraft. Elizabeth found this difficult, because of her own wholehearted, "no reserve and no delay" commitment to Christ; such inconsistency was not something she could easily accept. One of her colleagues, Dr Colin Fischbacher, spoke of the fact that few Malawians would say they do not believe in God, and yet at the same time they hold unto witchcraft. It is a deep-seated problem; people believe that everything is 'caused' by something, some demon. One Christian to whom Colin spoke said that he knew there were people who at night changed into hyenas and did various harmful things; the assertion was made in the same tones as a doctor might speak of there being a lot of chickenpox about just now. Part of the problem is that the church is unwilling to address the issue; even a chaplain called to counsel someone about Spiritism refused to attend, because he said the issue had nothing to do with him. When I raised the issue of how preachers would deal with a text such as 1 Corinthians 10, 21, "You cannot drink the cup of the Lord and the cup of demons too", I was told that they would tend not to choose such a text and, since expository preaching is not common, the issue would be left to one side.

It all highlights the need for more commitment to expository preaching from the Bible. This prevents preachers on the one hand from riding favourite hobbyhorses and, on the other, from avoiding difficult subjects. It may also raise the issue of whether we westerners, in different ways, weakly accept certain things that are inconsistent with biblical Christianity.

So far as the missionaries themselves are concerned, home churches can help by sending tapes of services; although, even then, missionaries do not always find it easy to actually sit down to listen.

Perhaps it was in view of some of these factors that Elizabeth was keen to make as much use of us as possible; she did not seem to think we were there for any kind of holiday! Indeed she kept up a frantic pace, never sitting down for very long. Even letter writing could be a daunting task: one day, when she was in Lilongwe, she posted a batch of letters she had written to friends and supporters at home; when she returned to Ekwendeni she found another 40 letters awaiting her; there were another 40 the next day. We hoped people understood when they didn't get a reply, or didn't hear from her for some time. She loved receiving the letters, and we used to try to encourage her simply to enjoy them without feeling guilty about not responding to every one.

Elizabeth kept us busy, conducting services and meetings in various places. It was a thrill to preach in the church where Elizabeth was an elder and very much part of the fellowship. In Ekwendeni itself, I was to preach one Sunday morning at the English-language service at 8 am. At about 7.55 am we looked into the church and saw that there were about four people present. This was an introduction to Malawian time-keeping or rather, a demonstration of the fact that the locals are not controlled by clocks; the Session Clerk said that we would simply wait until the people came. Gradually they drifted in, even after the service had started; eventually there was a congregation of several hundred.

We had heard that a minute book would be a useful gift, and we handed over a gilt-edged book that we had brought from home. Such was the outpouring of gratitude that a western observer might have thought that we had given the crown jewels - though they would have been much less useful. Sometimes a little can mean a lot.

On one of the other Sundays we were driven out to a "prayer house" at a village called Ekwliweni where I was to preach. The church was packed and people listened from outside; there must have been about 300 people, including about 50 children who sat at the front, on the ground, for all two and a half hours of the service; they had already been to Sunday School classes. The local minister interpreted for me, and it was there that I learned an interesting lesson in cultural adaptation. Elizabeth told me afterwards that he would slightly adapt my words. When, for example, I referred to unimportant material advantages, such as owning a car or a telephone, Elizabeth told me that Mr Hara had translated my words as: "You might have a suit..."

The intimations during the service included a "welcome address", when I was presented with a written greeting. It included the words: "We are pleased to see you - the first white minister to reach our church and preach the Word of God. We have learned you come from Scotland, the homeland of Dr David Livingstone and of our church". It was a great experience, leaving me feeling that if I had been the Moderator of the General Assembly, I could not have had a warmer or more enthusiastic welcome.

After the service, we were clapped all the way to the home of Mr Nkosi, a retired teacher, where we were to have lunch. We enjoyed chicken and *nsima* (maize porridge), followed by tea and sweet potato; Elizabeth, Nan and I discovered later that all three of us were struggling with the sweet potato, trying to "get it over" without offending our generous hosts! After more thanks, when it was mentioned that Ekwendeni usually keeps its visitors to itself, we and Elizabeth were all escorted back to her car in royal style.

Remembering our visit to Malawi, we look back on many other highlights. One such was the experience of meeting a family on the outward journey who were going to teach for a couple of years in a mission school in Nairobi, and hearing their 5-year old son saying: "**We**'re going to be missionaries"; not "my parents", but "we". On another occasion, having taken morning prayers at the hospital, I was thanked by the hospital evangelist who said: "We've had a wonderful day". It was only 7.30 in the morning! We enjoyed learning to barter rather than pay the stated price; one seller of wood carvings, asked about the price of a particular item, said: "The starting price is 160 kwacha"! A visit to Livingstonia and being able to look round the museum in the Stone House where Dr Laws once lived is bound to be a significant thing for Scots and we were no exception. Seeing a passenger on the 6 am Stagecoach to Lilongwe reading her Bible and apparently having her quiet time impressed us deeply; how often would such a thing be seen in Britain? Other memories include witnessing a wedding in Ekwendeni church, where there were 34 bridesmaids and 12 pageboys; custom dictated that neither the bride not bridegroom should smile during the proceedings! And who could forget sitting out in the sun during the, to us, warm, winter days of August? We were regarded as "crazy *azungu*" (Europeans) by passing Malawians who couldn't understand why anyone should wish to sit in the sun, and perhaps also by Elizabeth who was feeling the weather decidedly chilly.

The missionary retreat, which Elizabeth organised at Chikangawa has already been mentioned. This was a good time of fellowship, when I had the privilege of ministering God's Word several times and sharing the Lord's Supper with more than 20 missionaries. Such pastoral visits are much more easily arranged nowadays and we are sure that there is a great opportunity for such ministry and fellowship. It is greatly appreciated by overseas staff who often miss the depth of biblical teaching known in earlier years at home. Obviously tapes and CDs of services from home can be a great help.

Elizabeth's sister, Ruth, visited Malawi many times and was there when Elizabeth took ill. She also courageously paid a last visit some time after Elizabeth's death, when she was able to share the grief of the people of Ekwendeni.

Elizabeth's departure had been a hasty one, made in time of illness; there had been no opportunity for farewells or for expressions of thanks for her service, fellowship and friendship over her 15 years in Ekwendeni. Typical of the letters later received was one from a girl who thanked Elizabeth for being a good teacher, but also for "being a good mum to us".

The same note was struck by Kistone Mhango whose task as Primary Health Care Director (Preventive Health Department) involves overseeing 14 Community Based Health Care programmes: "The late Lizzie Mantell was our spiritual mother". Elizabeth was a great friend to Kistone and his wife Vesta and also to their children, Vitumbiko and Lusungu. Kistone recalls being on Elizabeth's khonde every Sunday after church for coffee and how Elizabeth was a frequent and welcome guest in their home. She was, he says, a kind of honorary mother-in-law:

> "...part and parcel of our family. She took care of us, especially Vesta, when we were expecting our firstborn baby."

Writing of her life, Kistone talks of prayer as a priority in Elizabeth's life, and he mentions three particular memories of her.

- She "encouraged all her students to attend Healthcare Christian Fellowship conferences at local, national and international levels, with her own financial support where appropriate";
- She used to "go round the wards and preach the word of God and many patients came to the saving knowledge of our Lord Jesus Christ";
- And at Easter "she used to organize a mountain climb nearby for the students and staff before sunrise. Thereafter she

prepared breakfast for everyone who participated in the service".

He also recalls that a favorite hymn of Elizabeth's was:
> I know not why God's wondrous grace to me He hath made known,
> Nor why, unworthy, Christ in love redeemed me for His own.
> But I know Whom I have believed and am persuaded that He is able
> To keep that which I've committed unto Him against that day.

This was a revelation to me; one of the verses of that hymn may now have an added significance:
> I know not what, of good or ill, may be reserved for me,
> Of weary ways or golden days before His face I see.

The word "mother" is one that seems to have attached itself to Elizabeth in the minds of many people in Malawi. Additional to those already mentioned, Sister Grace Mughogho, Hospital-Matron, writes of Elizabeth as:
> "A loving and caring mother not only to the hospital but also to the community; personally, the late Lizzie was precious to my family."

Finally, a memorial poem by Ellie Kapenda, begins by addressing her in similar terms:
> "Oh Mum! You are greatly missed by patients, clients and staff members of Ekwendeni Hospital. We do not forget your ever-smiling face to every individual, rich or poor. You loved your students. You loved openness and brought people together. Gossip was far from you; you cherished harmony."

Chapter 10
The Patient

When we heard in November 1996 that Elizabeth had been taken ill, it came as a shock. My wife and I had lived with her for the whole of August that year and had not noticed any particular problems. Occasionally she did speak of a discomfort in her abdomen but, when we went out for walks, she always strode forward as energetically and purposefully as was her normal style. Barbara Kwast, however, had noticed something.

She and Elizabeth had met, as recounted earlier, at Queen Charlotte's in London and their friendship lasted throughout Elizabeth's life. Barbara has written about a long weekend, which they shared at Lake Malawi, where they planned to read the book of Revelation together. Barbara writes,

> "I will never forget the quiet and reflective time in the beautiful scenery of the lake shore amidst God's creation: flowering frangipanis in various colors, lovely fragrances, once in a while a canoe coming with fresh fish, or Malawians walking along the beach from one village to the next. I remember vividly Elizabeth with her red hair among the flowering bougainvilleas and frangipanis – a little corner of paradise. Ever since Queen Charlotte's Hospital, Liz had through her quiet faith and humility an influence on me for which I am still thankful."

Early in 1995 Barbara visited Elizabeth at Ekwendeni; she found that the latter was due to go on furlough but that there was no one to take her place. Barbara offered to end her 30 years of service by spending three months tutoring at Ekwendeni. Then –

> "At the end of these three months (in August 1995), Elizabeth and I met at Amsterdam Airport, to 'hand over', as I left Malawi just before she returned to Ekwendeni. There was a disquiet in my heart when I met Elizabeth at the end of her furlough Was she really well and rested enough to return to Ekwendeni? I did not voice that, but I was worried. Great was my sadness when I heard of her illness and her return to Scotland in 1996."

That return was in November of that year. News spread that Elizabeth was ill and eventually that she was to be flown home. It was the beginning of a very difficult year, as various treatments were carried out in an attempt to arrest the growth of the tumour that was threatening her life.

GOD SO LOVED THE WORLD

Elizabeth Mantell, (Church of Scotland missionary), with a group of student nurses at Ekwendeni Hospital, Malawi – a hospital run by the Church of Central Africa Presbyterian

Later Elizabeth herself wrote of that *annus horribilis* that it was a time for her of great increase of faith and strength. One was reminded of the Apostle Paul's words in 2 Corinthians 4:16:

> "Therefore we do not lose heart. Though outwardly we are wasting away, yet inwardly we are being renewed day by day. For our light and momentary troubles are achieving for us an eternal glory that far outweighs them all. So we fix our eyes not on what is seen, but on what in unseen. For what is seen is temporal, but what is unseen is eternal."

Elizabeth received treatment first in the City Hospital in Edinburgh, and then in Aberdeen Royal Infirmary. Although many who visited her would hardly have realized it, this was a time when she was suffering considerable pain and discomfort. She wrote of how much the support and prayers of her many friends had meant to her:

Elizabeth 3rd from right with her father, mother, two sisters and her brother

Elizabeth's thoughts, of course, continued to be with Malawi, even as she was coming to terms with her own illness. As a patient in Aberdeen Royal Infirmary she learned that there was to be a change in uniform for the nurses there; dresses were to be replaced by blouses and trousers. This would mean that the old-style uniforms would be surplus to requirements; working in cahoots with hospital chaplain, the Rev Jim Falconer, she was instrumental in seeing that, before you could say "C.C.A.P. Hospital, Ekwendeni", no fewer than 1260 uniforms were duly packed and sent off to Ekwendeni. The April 1988 issue of *Foresterhill News & Views* reported:

"Staff at Ekwendeni Hospital in Malawi are now wearing the nurse uniforms donated by Aberdeen Royal Hospitals."

It reported on the receipt of a letter from Dr Chizizi, the Medical Superintendent at Ekwendeni, who said that the uniforms had arrived at just the right time as they had been struggling for funds to buy uniforms for the New Year. On Friday January 2nd 1998 the Evening Express reported:

"New-look North-east nurses have handed their old uniforms to a cash-strapped hospital in poverty-hit Africa. The donation means money that might have been spent on new uniforms can now be used for drugs to make the African hospital's AIDS patients – many of them babies – more comfortable in the days before their death. The generous move came by chance (!) while a nurse tutor from Ekwendeni was being treated at the

Granite City hospital. Macduff woman Elizabeth Mantell, a Church of Scotland missionary, said today, 'One of the hospital chaplains approached me and asked if we might be able to make use of the old uniforms. Malawi is very poor and the hospital, though better equipped than some, has a lack of resources and equipment. The uniforms were a wonderful gift. They saved us hundreds of pounds. They are already in Malawi and in use." Elizabeth, even in her terminal illness, was still looking out for Ekwendeni and would have credited God with the providential outcome.

In between courses of chemotherapy, she enjoyed a few holidays in Perth, after which she attended the Nurses' Christian Fellowship Conference in Crieff. Anne Dawson, who was then home on leave from Ekwendeni Girls' Secondary School, drove her to Lesley Thomson's commissioning service, and then she and Ruth enjoyed two good weeks at Achnahaird by Achiltibuie;

> "The weather was perfect for walking – and walking we did – amongst the hills, beside the lochs and along the cliff tops."

Shortly after this, she felt unwell again, and asked her correspondents,

> "As we go into the future, please continue to pray that I will be given the strength to cope with whatever it holds."

She enjoyed visits from Howard Kasiya, AIDS coordinator in Ekwendeni, and Esther Munthali. Like most African visitors, they found the climate in Scotland rather cold and wet, but they testified to the warmth of the welcome they enjoyed from many people. They brought reports of the worsening situation with AIDS in Malawi and sought prayer as they continued to fight to try to prevent the spread of the virus and as they nursed those with the disease.

Throughout this time, Elizabeth kept closely in touch with events at her beloved Ekwendeni. She rejoiced in the news that the Malawian government had supplied money for outstanding staff wages in the hospital; also on hearing that, for the following year, the Netherlands Government would support the Nursing School. She wrote of Carol Finlay's return in the previous February and her work in preparing the students for their exams, which would be held in October/November.

As the weeks went on, Elizabeth realised that she was seriously ill, and that the right thing to do was to resign from her missionary work.

She wrote again, evocatively, of the sounds and sights she missed and which she now knew she would never again experience.

"As I look out at the dull, dreich days, I think of the warm sunshine of Ekwendeni and realize with sadness that I may never experience that again. I will miss the sight of the villages, the far distant mountains and the beautiful flowering trees and bushes. I will miss the sound of the crickets at night, the frogs once the rain starts, the barking dogs, the chants and cries of the children. I will miss the smells of the first rains, the bushfires, the scent of the orange blossom, and so much else. All a memory now, but nonetheless a gift from God."

This was the prelude to her announcement of her retirement, on health grounds, to take effect at the end of December. It was on the Christmas Eve of that year that the local church's carol singing party stopped to sing outside 42 Low Shore and watched as a weakened Elizabeth managed to come to the door to listen, full of appreciation and delight at the traditional sound. It was only two days later that she was again taken into hospital. After a further month, on 27th January 1998, with Ruth and Harry at her bedside, Elizabeth slipped quietly and peacefully from life into death, and on to glory.

Writing to members of her own congregation in the Macduff church magazine, she had quoted the words of Philippians 1, 4-5: "In all my prayers for all of you I always pray with joy because of your partnership in the gospel from the first day until now", and had testified to her sadness that, after a year at home on sick leave, she was retiring from active missionary service. "It is now fifteen years since I went to Ekwendeni", she wrote, "and I want to thank all of you for your support over these years. This past year has been difficult, but your prayers have meant so much. Although I will no longer be in Ekwendeni, I know that you will still pray for the work there". She also expressed her pleasure at the fact that she would be staying in Macduff and would continue to share fellowship with her brothers and sisters there, although she perhaps did not realise then how short that time would be.

In her Partner Plan letter, addressed to her partner churches, particularly in the presbyteries of Buchan and Dunoon, Elizabeth expressed appreciation of the partnership she had received during her 15 years in Ekwendeni. She looked back on a period filled with challenge, excitement and some disappointments. She rejoiced in the new hospital which had become a reality; in having seen the nursing school develop into a training school for nurses and midwives; and in having watched the development of the Primary Health Care work with its many facets.

"Most important of all was seeing God's love continuing to grow amongst the people. There have been difficult times too, and your partnership and support in prayer and kind have enabled the work to continue through difficult as well as easy times. Thank you all."

The next official letter that came out from "121" (the Church of Scotland Offices in Edinburgh) was written by the then Partner Plan Secretary, Katy Laidlaw, who spoke of widespread sadness at Elizabeth's death. She wrote:

"Liz was a very special person and will be greatly missed. She was dearly loved both here and in Malawi. We are all mourning her passing, while glad that her pain and suffering are over. Her funeral was one of thanksgiving and praise for a life truly given to the service of others."

A sad part of Katy's letter was the reflection that, for congregations left without a Church of Scotland missionary partner, there was a shortage of people available. She wrote of a number of vacancies in various parts of the world and of money set aside to finance the posts, but without people to fill them. Clearly, the fact that Malawians are now leading much of the work of the mission hospital has a bearing on the situation; it is also known that there are many members of the Church of Scotland who are serving as missionaries with other missionary societies; but where is the supply of candidates to take up posts with our own church? Are there people today to answer the call to go out in service and mission to other lands? Consider the challenge of Frank Houghton's hymn:

> Facing a task unfinished,
> That drives us to our knees,
> A need that, undiminished,
> Rebukes out slothful ease,
> We who rejoice to know Thee
> Renew before Thy throne
> The solemn pledge we owe Thee
> To go and make Thee known.
>
> Where other lords beside Thee
> Hold their unhindered sway,
> Where forces that defied Thee
> Defy Thee still today,
> With none to heed their crying
> For life and love and light,
> Unnumbered souls are dying
> And pass into the night.

> We bear the torch that, flaming,
> Fell from the hands of those
> Who gave their lives, proclaiming
> That Jesus died and rose.
> Ours is the same commission,
> The same glad message ours;
> Fired by the same ambition,
> To Thee we yield our powers.

Where today are the young, and perhaps not so young, people who will step forward to answer the Lord's call to serve Him overseas? Of course the point can justifiably be made that the need in our own country is very great, yet it remains true that people here have many opportunities that are denied to others across the world. People here can go to a church if they want to find out more; they can obtain a Bible or other Christian literature; some can enquire of Christian friends. These are benefits denied to people in many parts of the world. Surely God still calls people to leave home and comforts to go overseas and serve others in His name?

Jim Elliot, whose ministry and martyrdom among the Quichua Indians of Ecuador has been read and re-read by many, was very forthright in his reflection on this call. Writing a letter to his parents, he said:

> "Consider the call from the Throne above, 'Go ye', and from round about, 'Come over and help us', and even the call from the damned souls below, 'Send Lazarus to my brothers, that they come not to this place', Impelled, then, by these voices I dare not stay home while Quichuas perish. So what if the well fed church in the homeland needs stirring? They have the Scriptures, Moses and the prophets, and a whole lot more. Their condemnation is written on their bank-books and in the dust on their Bible covers" ("Shadow of the Almighty", p. 134).

I remember the shock and disbelief I felt once, when, visiting in my parish, I met a lady who was on holiday. Somehow our conversation veered round to people's monetary donations to their churches, and she rather proudly mentioned the amount she gave every year. She gave the sum not weekly but once a year, in an envelope on which she wrote: "Not for missions"! She went on to express her view that missionaries lived in sufficient luxury and did not need more support. Some missionaries do feel that they enjoy a far higher standard of living than those among whom they live and work; they can sometimes be embarrassed about their comparative affluence; yet there can be no doubt that taking up missionary service almost always involves huge financial sacrifice.

James Denney's words may be apt; in one of his published sermons, he quoted a missionary as saying:

> "Some people say they do not believe in missions. They have no right to believe in missions. They do not believe in Christ."

Denney commented,

> "This goes to the root of the matter. It is not interest in missions that we want in our churches at this moment, but interest in the gospel. Apart from a new interest in the gospel, a revival of evangelical faith in Christ as Redeemer, I believe we shall look in vain for a response to missionary appeals" (The Way Everlasting, p.297).

Katy Laidlaw closed her letter:

> "'Thank You' seems inadequate for all that you did for Liz while she was in Ekwendeni and, more especially, in the months she was at home. She did appreciate your love, care and concern. I am sure, like me, you feel that it was a privilege to know her and that your life has been enriched through being one of her Partner Plan Correspondents during her years of service in Malawi."

During one of my visits to Elizabeth in hospital, she said, in a way that is perhaps typical of us canny Scots who don't wear our hearts on our sleeves: "If you ever have to take a service for me, I'd like it to be a joyful one". In the funeral service, we sought to honour that request; I spoke of making our sadness a kind of joyful sadness, as we gave thanks for the evidence of God's Spirit at work in Elizabeth's heart and life and rejoiced in the message of hope which was so real to her. One of the passages we read was Revelation 7:

> "After this I looked and there before me was a great multitude that no-one could count, from every nation, tribe, people and language, standing before the throne and in front of the Lamb...one of the elders asked me, 'These in white robes – who are they, and where did they come from?' And he said, 'These are they who have come out of the great tribulation; they have washed their robes and made them white in the blood of the Lamb. Therefore, "They are before the throne of God and serve him day and night in his temple; and he who sits on the throne will spread his tent over them. Never again will they hunger; never again will they thirst. The sun will not beat upon them, nor any scorching heat, For the Lamb at the centre of the throne will be their shepherd; he will lead them to springs of living water. And God will wipe away every tear from their eyes."

Such is the faith by which Elizabeth lived. At her bedside in hospital I remember reading the latter part Isaiah 40. I believe it was after hearing these words that she spoke of that year as being, for her, a time of great increase of faith:

> "The Lord is the everlasting God, the Creator of the ends of the earth. He will not grow tired or weary, and his understanding no-one can fathom. He gives strength to the weary and increases the power of the weak. Even youths grow tired and weary, and young men stumble and fall; but those who hope in the Lord will renew their strength. They will soar on wings like eagles; they will run and not be weary, they will walk and not faint."

A large company of people, many of who had travelled many miles to be there, attended Elizabeth's funeral service in Macduff Church. At the same time as the service was taking place in Macduff, another service was also taking place in Ekwendeni, of which a colleague, Dr Colin Dick, wrote later:

> "The service here on the day of the funeral was amazing with singing in Tumbuka that nearly lifted the roof off. It was a privilege to witness how much Liz was loved here."

Old Ekwendeni Church

Another account came from Grace Mughogho, a Malawian who was a close personal friend of Elizabeth's. She wrote:
"Ekwendeni church was far too small – people came in large numbers. Liz was not for Ekwendeni only but for the world and she was a caring mother for children all ages – difficult to find one like her."

Margaret Young, a missionary from the Presbyterian Church of Ireland, also wrote about the service held in Ekwendeni Church on the day of Elizabeth's funeral; she described it as very helpful for those who were feeling that Macduff was a long way away. Margaret wrote about the sadness caused in Ekwendeni by Liz's death; she felt that many Malawians hadn't accepted how ill Elizabeth really was. Margaret wrote:

> "I miss her badly, but it is also good to be able to give thanks that her suffering is over, and to know that she is with the Lord who was the focus of her life."

At the time of Elizabeth's funeral, her family decided to establish a Thanksgiving Account, to which people might be asked to contribute in lieu of flowers, etc. The esteem in which Elizabeth was held is shown by the fact that over £16,000 was donated. Most of this went to support the work in Ekwendeni, with smaller donations also for cancer research at Aberdeen Royal Infirmary, for Echo and for Macmillan Nurses.

Elizabeth's sister, Ruth, who died in February 2008 at the age of 86, was, as Joan Waldron recounts:

> "... another remarkable person – always a tower of strength all through Elizabeth's years in Africa, supporting her in so many ways, not least of which, of course, was spending months out there with her, doing all sorts of tasks to help;...Elizabeth looked up to her a lot."

Almost a year after Elizabeth's death, Ruth bravely paid a last visit to Ekwendeni, and found that Malawians were still feeling bereaved. In a circular to friends at home, Ruth wrote:

> "Do I regret coming? Definitely not, despite the sadness of not having Elizabeth and constantly remembering her working at the Nursing School and walking where we had often walked together birdwatching.... I knew from letters how sad they were at the news of Elizabeth's death but had not realized how deprived they felt at not being able to condole with any of her family as is the custom here. They came to see me in groups – the hospital staff, the Umanyano (Woman's Guild), the choir who sang a song especially written for Elizabeth's memorial service, the ministers, the domestic staff and many who came alone to sit quietly and tell what she has meant to them and what she had done for them. Some I knew well; others were people she had supported or advised when they had problems. They came to express their sorrow, to pray and to sing hymns, and to show their concern for Elizabeth's family and friends in Scotland."

So Elizabeth's earthly life came to a close – "too soon", many of us would say, but she herself would have us trust in One who is all wise, who knows the end from the beginning (Isaiah 46, 10) and who has his reasons for everything he does. He is also one who welcomes his faithful servants with a generous,

> "Well done, good and faithful servant; enter into the joy of your Lord."
> (Matthew 25:23)

As was suggested at the outset, Elizabeth herself would have been first amazed and then horrified at the thought of her story being written in a book. She did not have a high opinion of herself.

Yet it is here that one of her greatest strengths lay. She was all too aware of her weaknesses and would certainly have wanted any account of her life to be a "warts and all" account. She could be impatient sometimes, especially with bureaucracy, but also with people. Wilma Nicolson, who started nursing with Elizabeth in 1960 and remained a friend until the latter's death, could write about how:

> "Elizabeth shared freely her frustrations and irritations and tiredness as one can and should do to a close friend."

That impatience and tiredness were no doubt partly caused by her own high standards and failure to realize that not everyone could keep up with her! She expected much of herself and she expected much of other people. The sheer fatigue that has been noted elsewhere was another factor; in a January 1986 letter she wrote about being

> "So tired that poor John got the brunt of it all and then I had to go and apologize."

Much of that tiredness may have been brought on by herself, not only by her insistence on the high standards of professionalism by which she lived, but also by the busyness of the hospital, by her own prolific letter writing and by the open-hearted hospitality, which often left her exhausted.

But if Elizabeth had weaknesses, she had many strengths and we close this account of her life by mentioning four of them.

One was that self-effacing humility that was such a notable characteristic of her life and which endeared her to so many. She had no airs and graces and no high opinion of herself. It was perhaps this genuine humility that most characterized her personality. It was no put-on self-effacement of the kind lampooned in Coleridge's lines: "And the Devil did grin, for his darling sin is pride that apes humility". Elizabeth was genuinely unassuming and had no idea that she was anything special.

A second characteristic was her long-term commitment. It had been her lifelong ambition to care for babies in Africa and she committed herself to that task. This is not to imply that she regarded the ten-year period during which she looked after her mother as any kind of interruption or irritation. There was no such thought in Elizabeth's mind at all; indeed, later, when Edith McKay, a fellow-elder in Macduff, was visiting Ekwendeni and casually asked whether there was anything that would bring her home from Africa, her immediate reply was:

> "If Ruth needed me"! She lived out the principle of 1 Timothy 5:8 where Paul bluntly lays it down: "If anyone does not provide for his relatives, and especially for his immediate family, he has denied the faith and is worse than an unbeliever."

Still, she had a long-term commitment. In recent times there has been a growth in the number of people giving short-term service overseas and it is wonderful that many are prepared to give part of their life and career to serve in areas of poverty and need. Elizabeth, however, represented the band of people for whom commitment is a long-term affair. As has been noted in this book, life for her in Ekwendeni was not at all easy, but she was "in it for the long haul". Her heart was in Africa; when she returned in 1983, she began a letter with the statement:

> "I have now been back in Malawi for four days and it seems in some ways that I have never left it."

Both the window in Macduff Church and the circulation of this written account will help ensure that Elizabeth will not be forgotten. However, many friends and admirers do not need either; her real legacy, of course, is in the lives of Malawian people. It was during her terminal illness that Elizabeth expressed to Ruth the hope that "they won't forget Ekwendeni". Ekwendeni has not been forgotten. Congregations in Scotland remember the mission there in many ways; at the time of writing, over £2000 has recently been raised in a single effort in Macduff for the provision of a deep bore well for the Ekwendeni district. Many similar efforts have been, and are being, made to maintain and strengthen the links between Scotland and Malawi.

The Raven Trust, a charity organised with indefatigable energy by John and Sue Challis of Strachur, undertakes another admirable work. They say of Elizabeth:

> "What an incredible inspiration she was to all of us – Raven Trust exists because of her."

Sue writes:

> "Even now, when I am tired and want to walk away from all the busyness of the Trust her words come back to me – "Don't forget Ekwendeni" – and somehow the strength and inspiration to carry on returns."

John and Sue met Elizabeth through the Church of Scotland's Partner Plan. Elizabeth was the link missionary for their congregation for many years. There, they recall: "The interest in her work was rather less than we were happy with and I admit we stirred things up a bit". Elizabeth also invited them to visit her at Ekwendeni.

> "I said, 'Yes' and gave her a date when I hoped to arrive and left it at that. When I turned up at Ekwendeni on the said date, she wasn't expecting me – usually visitors send a list of questions etc, before arrival; I just took the local bus – but her welcome (after the initial shock) was happy and warm. Even though she was in the middle of exams for the students."

What is their memory of Liz?

> "Kind, funny, stern, professional, challenging and a good friend – although I would have been a bit scared to be one of her students!"

The Raven Trust continues with the wonderful work of sending large containers to Malawi filled with all manner of useful things. Their website is well worth a visit it tells us that over the past few years container loads have been transported to Africa with goods with an estimated value in excess of £1,000,000. Provisions sent out recently included:

> Medical Supplies (basic hospital disposables such as gloves, bandages, dressings, needles, syringes etc. Also equipment such as Ultra-scan machines, operating tables, infusion pumps, x-ray equipment, operating instruments, ECG machines & patient monitors)
>
> Books and Videos (medical, educational, secular and theological)
>
> Tools and Equipment (carpentry tools, saw bench and planes, metal working tools, computers, printers, cables & monitors etc)

Clothing (knitted goods for babies, blankets, cotton sheets, clothing etc)

Toiletries (soap, talc, shampoo & disposable razors)

Other items include mattresses, footballs, netballs, sports equipment, football strips, stationery, lecturing equipment, a ship's engine and children's playgroup toys.

And all of it, as the Challises say, happens because of Elizabeth.

Among her home congregation Elizabeth's hope that Ekwendeni should not be forgotten has been honoured. No midweek service goes past without Ekwendeni being prayed for, along with other mission partners; it has also been a joy to welcome to Scotland various Malawian visitors including Kistone Mhango, Esther Mwafalirwa and Howard Kasiya. When Macduff Church celebrated its Bicentenary in 2005, it was decided that the thank offering (£1300) should be given to Ekwendeni and, when our Session Clerk and his wife celebrated their silver wedding in 2006, they requested that, in lieu of personal gifts, donations might be sent to a special fund for Ekwendeni. As a result, the sum of £2025 was raised, increased by Gift Aid to £2325.38. No, Ekwendeni has not been forgotten; may the work there continue to be remembered by the people of Scotland.

The third major feature of Elizabeth's life and character was her love for other people. She was, quite simply, a caring person. That has been shown in earlier stories of the help she gave to others, often in very quiet and even secretive ways. Many stand in debt to the generosity of this quiet, Scottish lassie who simply cared for other people.

Of course, the other strength of her life was her faith, that faith in Christ which expressed itself in her life of commitment. That love of Christ has been evident throughout this story of Elizabeth's life, whether depicted in her ministering with her Bible in one hand and a bag of sugar in the other to a dying African woman; or getting up during the night to help African women experiencing difficult labours; or in caring for members of her own family; or showing love in her district work in Macduff, whether as a nurse or an elder. Behind it all stood her faith in the Lord, that faith which had been implanted in her in early days and which sustained her through difficult as well as happy times. She testified often to the truth of her life-text, "My grace is sufficient for you". As a friend, Douglas Willis, has written, she would have hated anyone to think there was anything angelic or saintly about the way she lived her life.

"She did what she did because she'd come to serve the Lord who had called her to work on His behalf in that challenging African situation"

This is echoed by Dr John Dorward's appreciation:

"Elizabeth, Liz, Sister Mantell or Auntie Liz – everyone's friend. She brought her skills, her warm personality and her sincere faith to two hospitals in Malawi and had an immeasurable impact over 20 years as a missionary from the Church of Scotland. Her life in Malawi epitomized all that the Christian pilgrimage should be – God-centered and Christ-glorifying in practical, humble living".

Many people in Scotland and Malawi, and doubtless in other places too, would echo the simple eloquence of the concluding line of another letter from friends Arthur and Mary Buck:

"We shall never forget Elizabeth. She was our friend.

www.ingramcontent.com/pod-product-compliance
Lightning Source LLC
Chambersburg PA
CBHW010717300426
44114CB00021B/2880